Second Edition

Antique Jewelry

WITH PRICES

Doris J. Snell

Published by

**krause
publications**

**700 E. State Street • Iola, WI 54990-0001
Telephone: 715/445-2214**

Please call or write for our free catalog of publications.
Our toll-free number to place an order or obtain a free catalog is 800-258-0929
or please use our regular business telephone 715-445-2214
for editorial comment and further information.

Library of Congress Catalog Number: 87-50013

ISBN: 0-87069-756-0

1 2 3 4 5 6 7 8 9 0 6 5 4 3 2 1 0 9 8 7

Cover design by Anthony Jacobson
Cover photo by Donna Chiarelli
Text photos by Charles Gehret Studio

Printed in the United States of America

This second edition is dedicated to my husband Robert, Teddy, Miss Bunney, T.P., and the gang. It is compiled in memory of my son Alexander, my parents Alexander and Louise Karas (Gettysburg, Pennsylvania), and my mentor Byron Haverly-Blackford (Bellefonte, Pennsylvania).

Acknowledgments

I wish to thank the staff of Krause Publications for giving me the opportunity to prepare a second edition of this book. If I knew all of their names, you may be sure I would mention them here.

Contents

Introduction

The purpose of this book continues to be that of an instant compact reference that reflects realistic current market values for collectible antique jewelry.

This second edition contains updated prices for each item illustrated in **Section I**. A completely new **Section II** has been added. This addition covers baby jewelry, Days of the Week cameo bracelets, eyeglass chains, lingerie clasps, mens' jewelry, and sword pins. Please refer to the expanded Table of Contents on page 5. Note also the addition of a section covering Masonic and Eastern Star Jewels.

Other helpful facts have been included in the Appendix: Gold marks, abbreviations, weights, alloy compositions, a monogram alphabet to help the reader identify the letters engraved on antique jewelry, Art Nouveau designs currently being used in revival and/or reproduced jewelry, and wrist watch dial styles helpful in dating, at a glance, watches sold during the 1930s.

The spelling of hand-carved Italian shell cameos has been revised to coincide with the exact spelling used in a 1970s cameo factory sales catalog. The words rosaline, cornilian, and sardonic replace the words rosalyn, cornelian, and sardonyx. With the advent in recent years of laser-carved cameos, older shell cameos will rapidly increase in value.

Bracelets

Scotch agate, links,
rolled gold trim
$400

Garnets set in
rolled gold plate
$210

Garnets,
rolled gold plate
$425

Gold-filled
$200

Less than 10k gold,
ruby
$225

Gold-filled
$210

Bride's bracelet,
garnets, gold-filled
$225

Bride's bracelet,
garnets, gold-filled
$225

Gold-filled,
black enameling
$200

Assorted bracelets, circa 1860-1890.

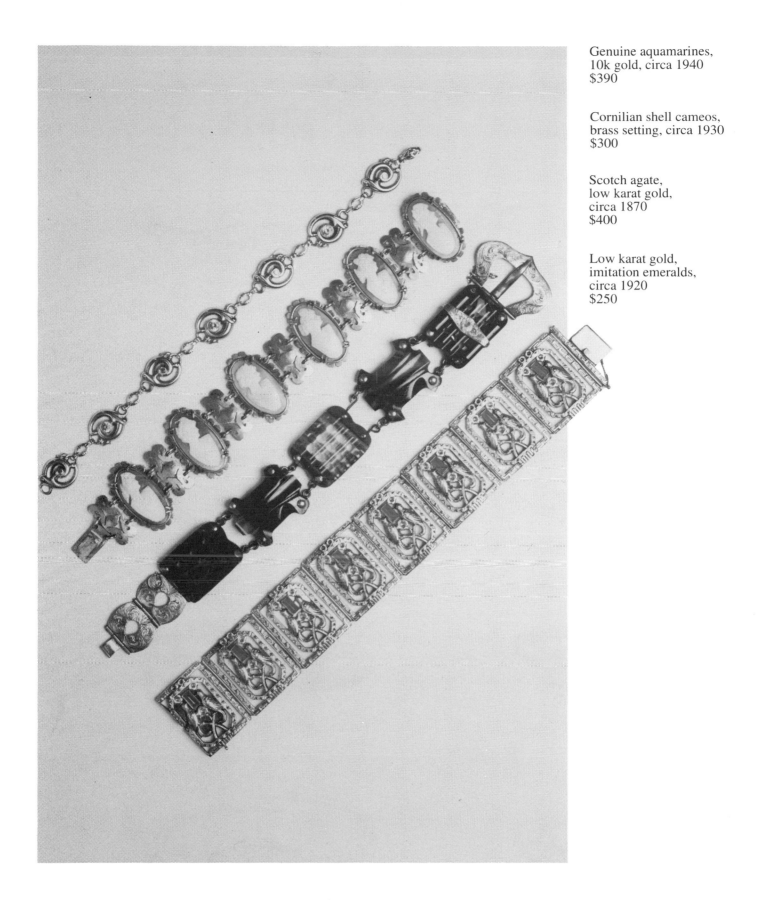

Genuine aquamarines,
10k gold, circa 1940
$390

Cornilian shell cameos,
brass setting, circa 1930
$300

Scotch agate,
low karat gold,
circa 1870
$400

Low karat gold,
imitation emeralds,
circa 1920
$250

These four bracelets show style changes that took place from Victorian to modern days.

Engraved, 1/2" width
$175

Engraved 3/8" width
$185

Engraved, 1/4" width
$145

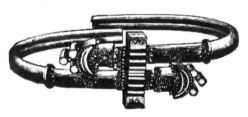

Engraved, 1/4" width
$175

Ornamented
$175

Garnets and pearls
$275

Ornamented
$185

Ornamented
$200

Ornamented
$195

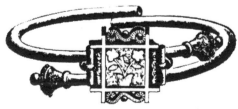

Ornamented
$185

Bracelets, circa 1889, all rolled gold plate.

10

$90

$90

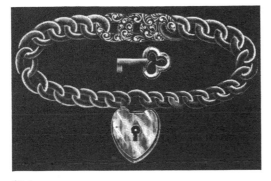

$95

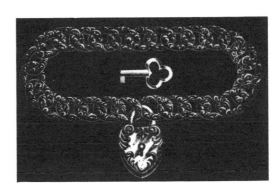

$95

$110

$110

$110

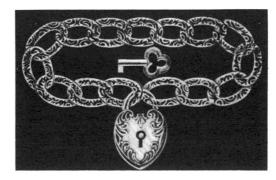

$95

Gold-filled bracelets, circa 1896.

Rose gold-filled,
coral cameo
$250

Rose gold-filled,
rhinestone in mouth
$275

Sterling silver,
gray finish
$125

$130

Four amethysts,
two rhinestones
$225

Pearl, eight sapphires,
six rhinestones, each side
$175

$90

$175

Sterling silver
$125

Bracelets, circa 1917, yellow gold-filled
unless otherwise identified.

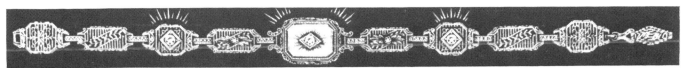

Frosted crystal and brilliants
$120

Brilliants and imitation crystal
(exact copy of a platinum and diamond bracelet)
$110

Imitation blue sapphires and brilliants
$110

Imitation peridot
$125

Imitation amethysts
$125

Sterling with rhodium finish,
imitation onyx, brilliants
$120

Imitation blue sapphires and brilliants
$120

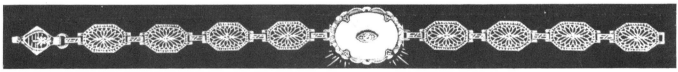

Sterling silver with rhodium finish,
frosted crystal, and brilliants
$110

Rose-colored glass stones
$95

Bracelets, circa 1932, rhodium mountings,
except where indicated.

Imitation emerald and brilliants
$115

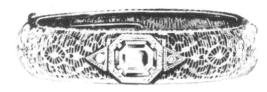

Crystal and brilliants
$125

Brilliants
$100

Frosted crystal and brilliants
$125

Rhodium, frosted crystal,
and brilliants
$120

Sterling with chrome finish,
imitation sapphires
$135

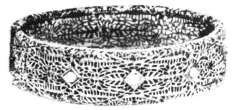

Sterling with chrome finish,
brilliants
$120

White gold plate,
imitation blue sapphires
$125

White gold plate
imitation blue sapphires,
and brilliants
$90

Rhodium with imitation
emerald baguettes
$85

Rhodium with crystal baguettes
$85

Chrome, pink glass stones
and brilliants
$95

Bracelets, circa 1932, rhodium mountings,
except where indicated.

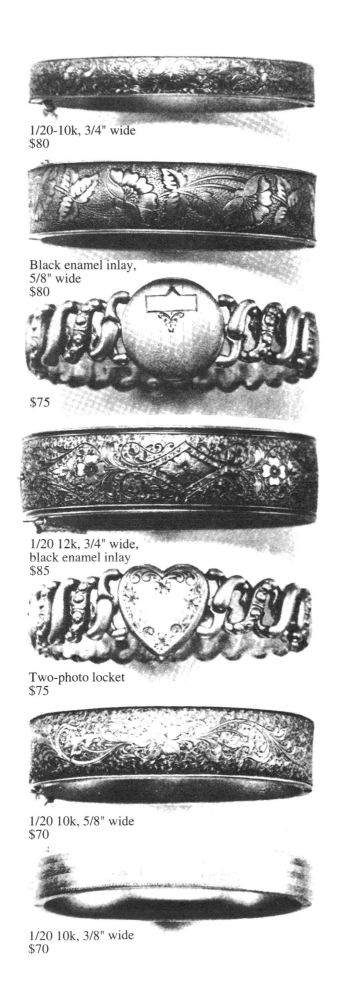

1/20-10k, 3/4" wide
$80

Black enamel inlay,
5/8" wide
$80

$75

1/20 12k, 3/4" wide,
black enamel inlay
$85

Two-photo locket
$75

1/20 10k, 5/8" wide
$70

1/20 10k, 3/8" wide
$70

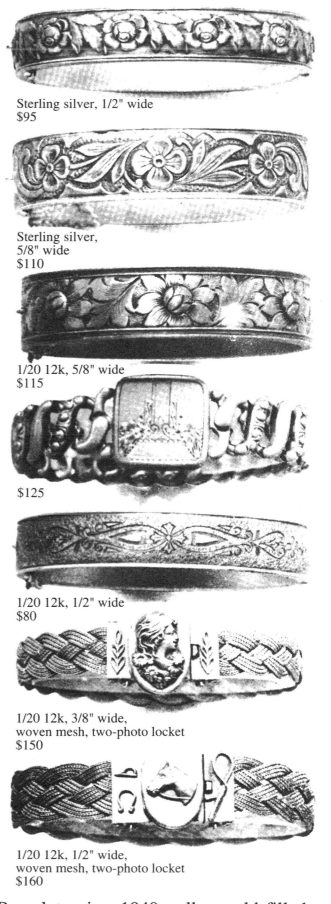

Sterling silver, 1/2" wide
$95

Sterling silver,
5/8" wide
$110

1/20 12k, 5/8" wide
$115

$125

1/20 12k, 1/2" wide
$80

1/20 12k, 3/8" wide,
woven mesh, two-photo locket
$150

1/20 12k, 1/2" wide,
woven mesh, two-photo locket
$160

Bracelets, circa 1940, yellow gold-filled,
except where indicated.

Woven mesh
$110

Woven mesh
$95

Woven mesh
$130

Woven mesh, simulated pearl,
black enamel inlay
$115

Plain and engraved links
$85

Gold-filled green leaves,
gold-filled red flowers
$85

Gold-filled red and green flowers
$80

Gold-filled green leaves,
gold-filled red flowers
$70

Plain and engraved links
$70

Bracelets, circa 1941, all yellow gold-filled.

Red and green gold-filled
$75

Black onyx, diamond
$85

Red and green gold-filled
$85

Cornilian cameo
$135

Red and green gold-filled
$85

Cuff-style bracelets, circa 1941, gold-filled.

$75

Oynx,
genuine cultured pearl
$75

$75

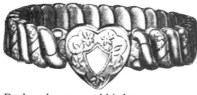

Red and green gold inlay
$75

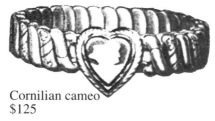

Cornilian cameo
$125

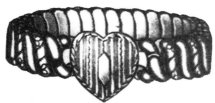

Red and green gold inlay
$75

$60

Mother of pearl cameo
$125

$70

Green gold inlay
$70

Green gold inlay
$75

Red and green gold overlay
$75

$60

Bracelets and lockets, circa 1942, yellow gold-filled.

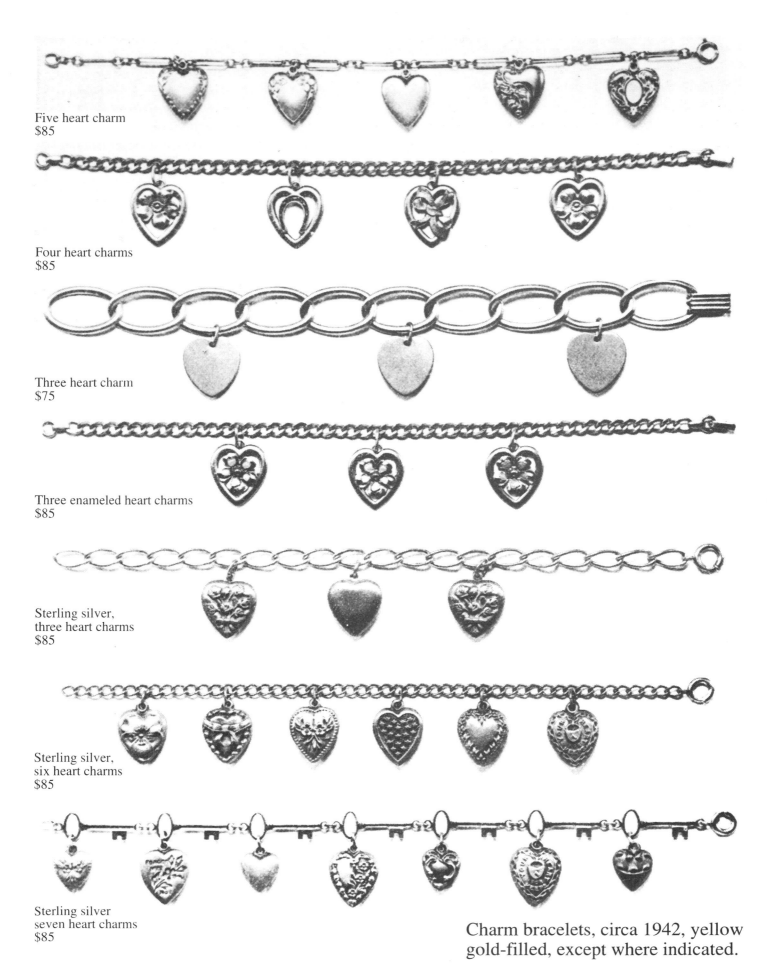

Five heart charm
$85

Four heart charms
$85

Three heart charm
$75

Three enameled heart charms
$85

Sterling silver,
three heart charms
$85

Sterling silver,
six heart charms
$85

Sterling silver
seven heart charms
$85

Charm bracelets, circa 1942, yellow
gold-filled, except where indicated.

19

Three imitation zircons
$85

Three genuine carved jade stones
$110

Three rose diamonds in genuine black onyx
$135

Three cornilian shell cameos
$135

Cornilian shell cameo
$125

Two-tone finish,
three zircons
$90

Sterling, five genuine zircons
$85

Genuine zircon
$70

Two-tone finish,
eight cultured pearls
$65

Bracelets, circa 1943, yellow gold-filled,
except where indicated.

Brooches and Pins

$110

$110

$120

$120

$120

$145

$190

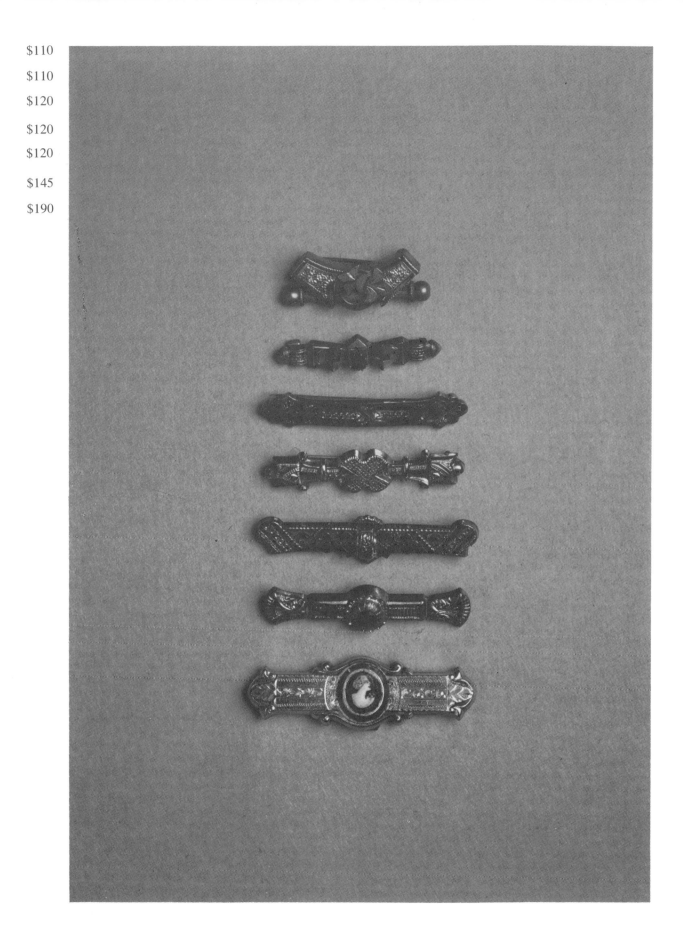

Bar pins, circa 1870-1900. Fronts are rolled
gold; backs are brass.

$175

$175

$175

$175

Victorian hollowware brooches, circa
1860-1880, have low karat gold fronts.

Brooch,
gold-filled, painting on
porcelain
$225

Chatelaine (watch) pin,
gold-filled
$175

Chatelaine (watch) pin,
14k gold
$300

Chatelaine (watch) pin,
gold
$325

Chatelaine (watch) pin,
gold-filled, garnet
$140

Chatelaine (watch) pin,
gold
$275

Gold front, garnet
$150

Gold front, applied design
$150

Gold front
$150

Gold, garnets
$250

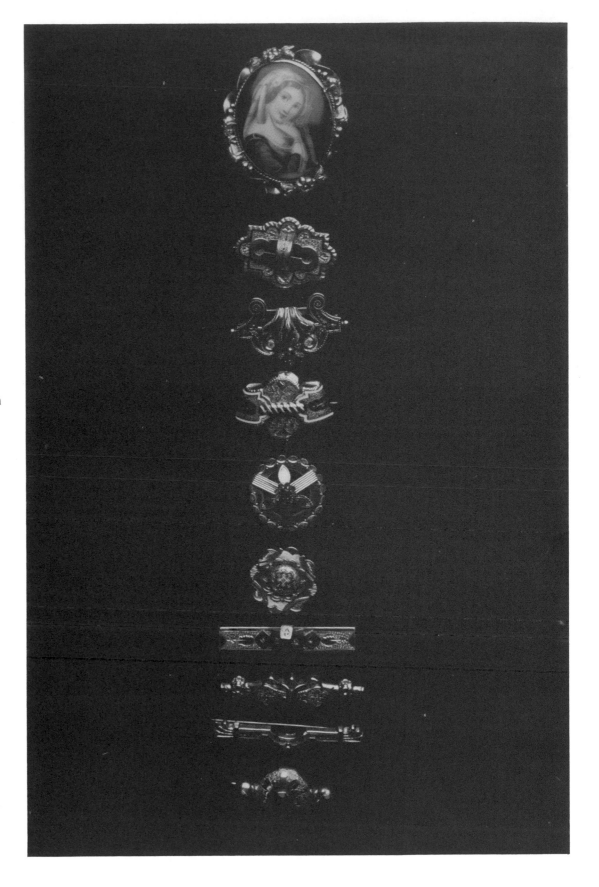

Brooches and pins, circa 1880-1900.

Lava cameo,
low karat gold setting
$575

Intaglio,
low karat gold setting
$175

Human hair,
14k findings
$325

Brooches and cross, circa 1870-1890.

1840-1850
Painting on porcelain
$225

Pre-1840
Artist signed painting, reset in late
1800s in a brass back with marcasites
on upper border
$450

1870-1890
Mosaic in low karat gold setting
$375

$90

$90 $90

$90

Brooches, circa 1900-1920, hand-painted
porcelain with brass settings or backs.

Reversible,
gold, human hair on one side,
picture on the other,
1870-1885
$600

Mosaic, low karat setting,
1879-1890
$350

Topaz, sapphires, low karat gold,
1870-1880
$450

Rolled gold plate, black enameling,
1880-1890
$150

Low karat gold, black enameling,
1870-1880
$175

Goldstone, low karat gold setting,
1880-1890
$140

Gold plated,
1870-1880
$110

Gold plated, imitation garnets
and sapphire,
1880-1890
$140

Rolled gold plate, blue and
black enameling,
1880-1890
$175

Yellow 14k gold, pearls
$175

Yellow 10k gold, amethyst
$225

Yellow 14k gold, aquamarine
$175

Yellow 10k gold, amethyst
$150

White 10k gold
$175

White 14k gold, blue sapphire
$175

White 10k gold
$150

White 10k gold, blue sapphire
$210

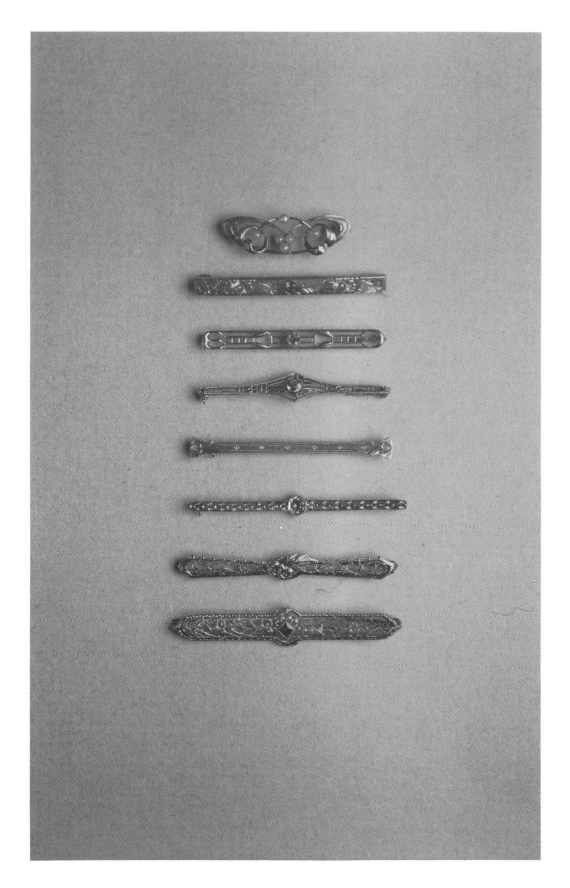

Bar pins, circa 1905-1915.

Imitation amethyst
$80

Imitation amethyst
$90

Painted porcelain
$140

Painted porcelain, tiny imitation amethysts
$140

$50

Brooches (also called sash pins)
with gold-plated settings,
circa 1900-1920.

Gold-filled setting,
1920-1930
$175

Seed pearls,
1890-1910
$200

French,
1890-1900
$200

Painted porcelain brooches from various
periods.

Coral cameo
$250

Branch coral
$150

Coral, black onyx
$150

Branch coral converted to a pendant
$250

Brooches and earrings, circa 1870-1890, low karat gold.

Painted porcelain
$125

Painted porcelain
$150

Painted porcelain
$200

Reverse painting on glass
$200

Brooches, circa 1930,
with gold plated settings.

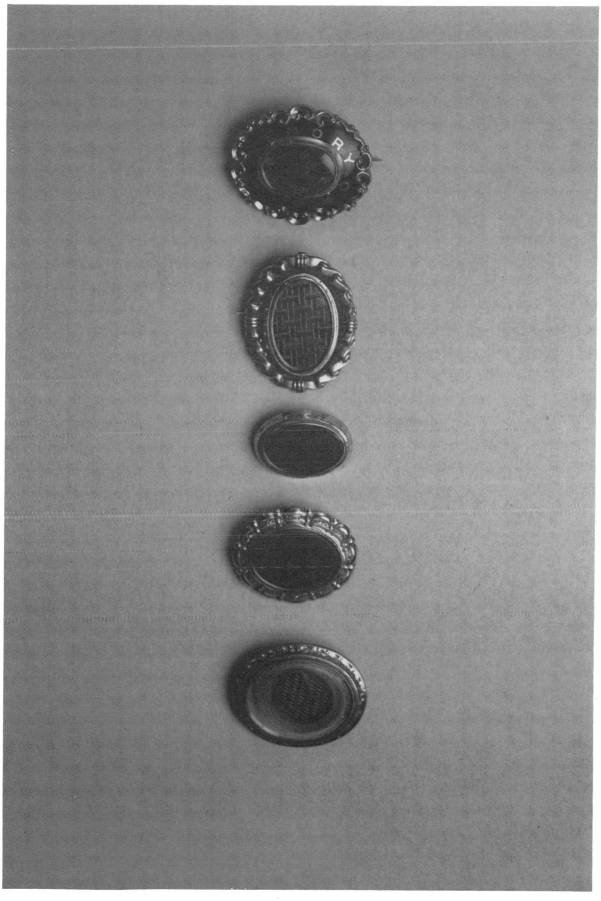

Gold, human hair,
1870-1885
$350

Reversible,
gold, human hair,
1880-1900
$275

Gold, human hair,
1880-1900
$210

Gold, human hair,
1880-1900
$325

Gold, human hair,
1880-1900
$300

Goldstone, gold plated,
1880-1890
$65

Watch pin,
gold -filled,
1900-1910
$85

Gold-filled,
1900-1915
$125

Watch pin,
gold-filled,
1910-1920
$95

Gold plated,
1900-1910
$100

Low karat gold,
1890-1900
$125

Turn-of-the-century brooches and watch pins.

Hand-painted ivory, sterling setting
$190

Painted ivory, sterling
$190

Painted ivory, sterling
$190

Painted ivory, sterling
$225

Pendant
painted ivory,
sterling with gold plating
$225

Post-1950 brooches and pendant shown
are often mistaken for antique jewelry.
Such items are readily available in Italy today.

$110

$110

$110

$120

$110

$95

$120

$95

$120

$95

$120

$95

Bar pins, circa 1885, rolled gold plate.

$145

$145

$145

$125

$125

$145

$140

$120

Bar pins, circa 1885, engraved gold fronts.

$80

$95

$85

$85

$95

$95

$95

$95

$95

$95

$95

$95

$100

$95

$95

$95

$100

$95

$95

$95

$95

$95

$85

Chatelaine pins, circa 1910. All are 1/10 14k gold-filled.

Sterling with non-
tarnishable chromium
finish, one brilliant in
basket setting and
two emeralds
$50

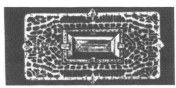

Non-tarnishable
white finish,
light green
imitation olivine
stone
$50

Non-tarnishable
white finish,
two brilliants
and an imitation
zircon
$50

Rhodium, frosted
crystal, one brilliant
imitation onyx
$50

Sterling with non-
tarnishable chromium
finish, one brilliant in
basket setting
$50

Sterling with
rhodium finish,
imitation crystal and
one brilliant stone
$50

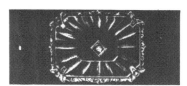

Non-tarnishable
white metal
imitation emerald
$55

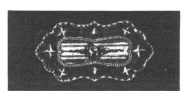

Sterling with
enameled center
$55

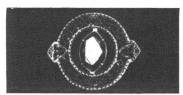

Sterling,
deep green zircon
$55

White 14k gold filled
with rhodium finish,
one brilliant, imitation
crystal, and onyx
$50

Sterling with
rhodium finish,
five brilliants
$55

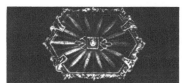

Rhodium plated on
white metal, one
brilliant, imitation
crystal
$50

Non-tarnishable
white metal,
imitation amethyst
$50

Sterling with
rhodium finish,
imitation emerald
$50

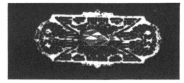

Non-tarnishable
white metal,
light green
imitation emerald
$55

Art Deco brooches, circa 1932.

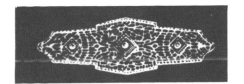

White 10k gold,
three diamonds
$170

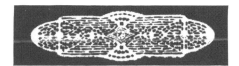

White 10k gold,
one diamond
$140

White 10k gold,
crystal, one diamond,
and black enameling
$190

White 14k gold,
one diamond
$135

White 14k gold,
one diamond,
four blue sapphires
$200

White 10k gold,
one diamond
$170

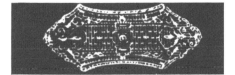

White 10k gold,
one diamond,
two sapphires
$185

White 10k gold,
applied 18k red and
green gold flowers,
synthetic Ceylon sapphire
$200

White 10k gold,
genuine frosted
crystal and one
diamond
$185

White 10k gold,
black onyx and
one diamond
$210

White 10k gold,
applied 18k red and
green gold flowers,
one synthetic emerald
$200

White 10k gold,
applied 18k red and
green gold flowers,
synthetic zircon
$195

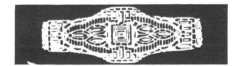

White 10k gold,
one diamond,
two blue sapphires
$190

White 10k gold,
one diamond
$190

White 14k gold,
one diamond
$140

White 10k gold,
one diamond and two
heart-shaped sapphires
$250

White 10k gold,
one diamond
$170

White 10k gold,
one diamond,
two emeralds
$225

Art Deco brooches, circa 1932.

$50

$55

$50

$55

$60

$50

$60

$55

$95

$125

Art Moderne sterling brooches and bracelets,
circa 1941.

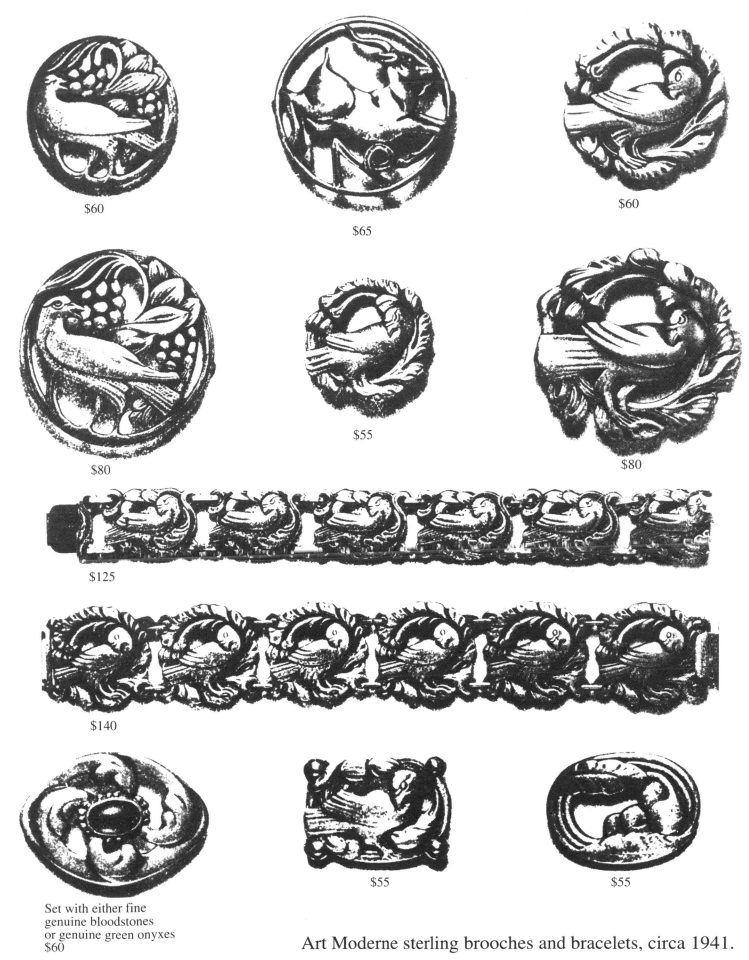

$60

$65

$60

$80

$55

$80

$125

$140

Set with either fine
genuine bloodstones
or genuine green onyxes
$60

$55

$55

Art Moderne sterling brooches and bracelets, circa 1941.

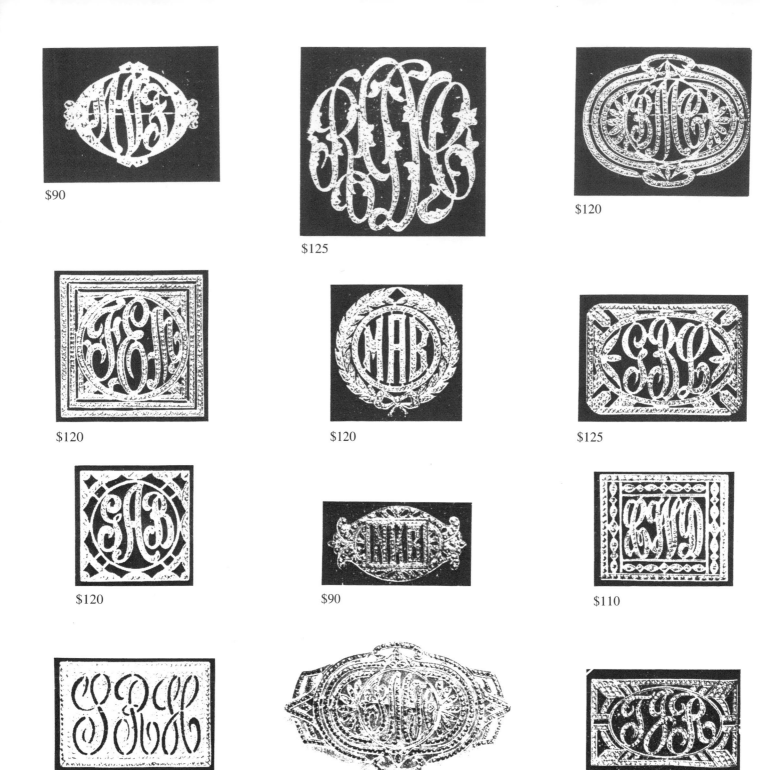

$90

$125

$120

$120

$120

$125

$120

$90

$110

$110

$125

$110

Art Moderne monogram brooches, circa 1941.
All are sterling silver with hand set French
marcasites.

44

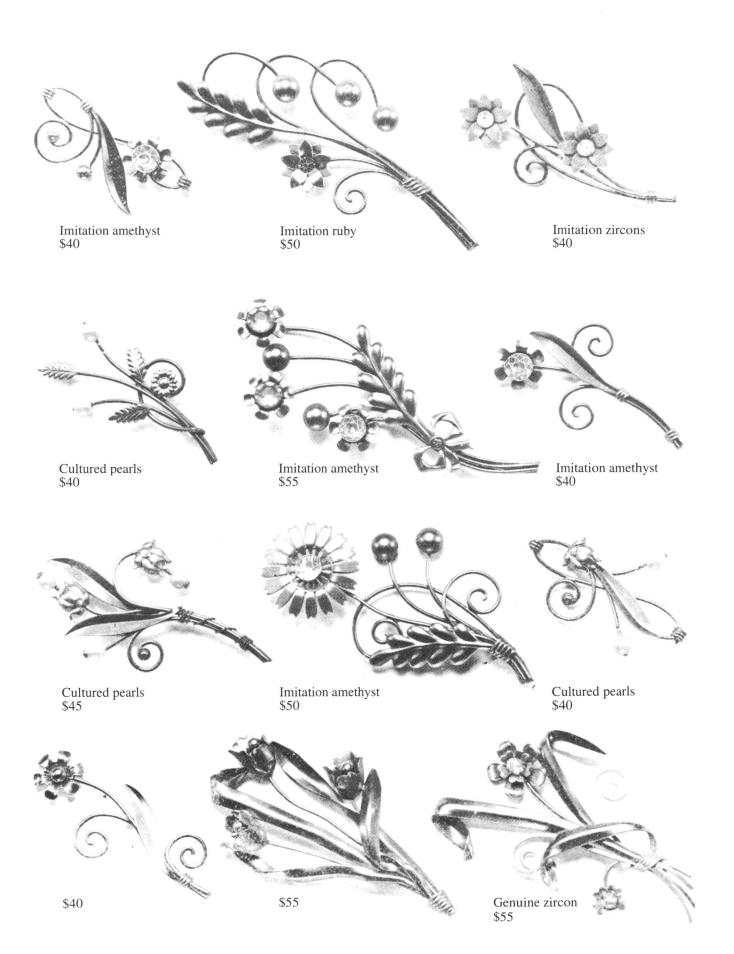

Imitation amethyst
$40

Imitation ruby
$50

Imitation zircons
$40

Cultured pearls
$40

Imitation amethyst
$55

Imitation amethyst
$40

Cultured pearls
$45

Imitation amethyst
$50

Cultured pearls
$40

$40

$55

Genuine zircon
$55

Brooches, circa 1943, gold-filled.

Cameo Jewelry

Pendant
rosaline shell cameo,
gold-filled setting,
1900-1920
$160

Brooch-Pendant
cornilian shell cameo,
low karat gold,
1930-1940
$240

Brooch
yellow 10k gold
sardonic shell cameo,
1935-1945
$395

Pendant
cornilian shell cameo,
low karat gold setting,
1930-1940
$225

Brooch
cornilian shell cameo,
gold plated setting,
pre-1925
$175

Brooch
cornilian shell cameo,
gold plated setting,
pre-1925
$145

Cornilian, rosaline and sardonic shell cameo brooches and pendants, circa 1900-1940.

Yellow 10k gold
rosaline shell cameo
$290

Yellow 10k gold
rosaline shell cameo
$350

Yellow 14k gold
sardonic shell cameo
$400

Yellow 10k gold
sardonic shell cameo
$450

Yellow 14k gold
cornilian shell cameo
$425

Shell cameo brooches, circa 1935-1945.

Cornilian shell cameo,
sterling
$215

Sardonic shell cameo,
sterling
$165

Sardonic shell cameo
$165

Pictured are three examples of shell cameo
brooches that were made sometime after 1950.

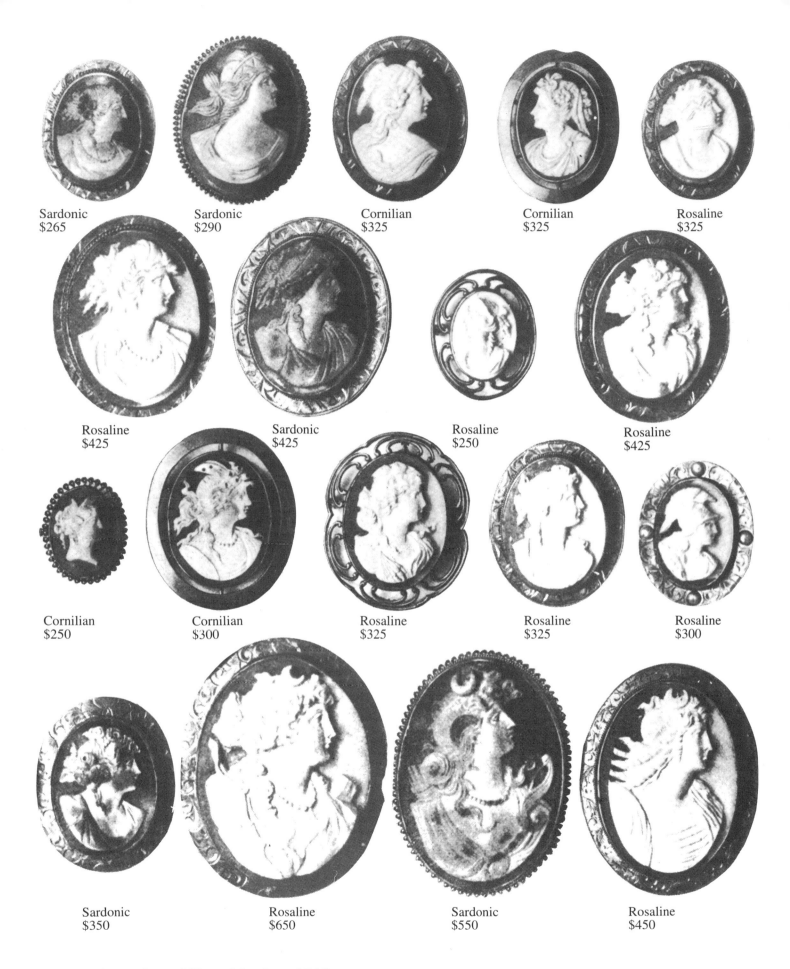

Sardonic
$265

Sardonic
$290

Cornilian
$325

Cornilian
$325

Rosaline
$325

Rosaline
$425

Sardonic
$425

Rosaline
$250

Rosaline
$425

Cornilian
$250

Cornilian
$300

Rosaline
$325

Rosaline
$325

Rosaline
$300

Sardonic
$350

Rosaline
$650

Sardonic
$550

Rosaline
$450

Cameo brooches, 10k gold, circa 1913.

White 10k gold,
applied 18k red
and green gold
flowers, cornilian
$275

White 14k gold,
one fine diamond,
cornilian
$200

Yellow 10k gold,
pink rosaline cameo
has a pendant ring
at top
$200

White 10k gold,
applied 18k red
and green gold
flowers, cornilian
$250

White 10k gold,
cornilian shell
$275

White 14k gold,
cornilian
$225

White 10k gold,
cornilian
$225

Sterling,
cornilian
$225

Sterling,
cornilian
marcasite frame
$125

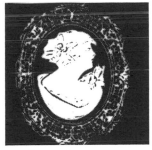

Sterling and
chromium,
cornilian, has
pendant ring
$150

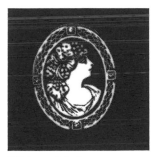

White gold plate,
four emeralds,
cornilian
$150

Sterling and
rhodium,
cornilian
$125

Cameo brooches, circa 1932.

| Yellow 10k gold, sardonic cultured pearl $200 | Yellow 10k gold, cornilian $125 | Yellow 10k gold, sardonic seed pearl frame $200 | Yellow 10k gold, cornilian $150 | Yellow 10k gold, cornilian plain frame $125 |

| Yellow 10k gold, cornilian two-tone frame $225 | Yellow 10k gold, cornilian two diamonds $250 | Yellow 10k gold, cornilian $250 | Yellow 10k gold, cornilian four diamonds $225 | Yellow 10k gold, cornilian $200 |

 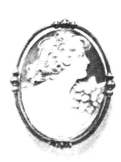   

| Gold-filled, cornilian marcasites $125 | Gold-filled, sardonic $150 | Gold-filled, cornilian $200 | Gold-filled, cornilian one diamond $150 | Gold-filled, cornilian $175 |

Cameo brooches, circa 1941.

Chains and Watches

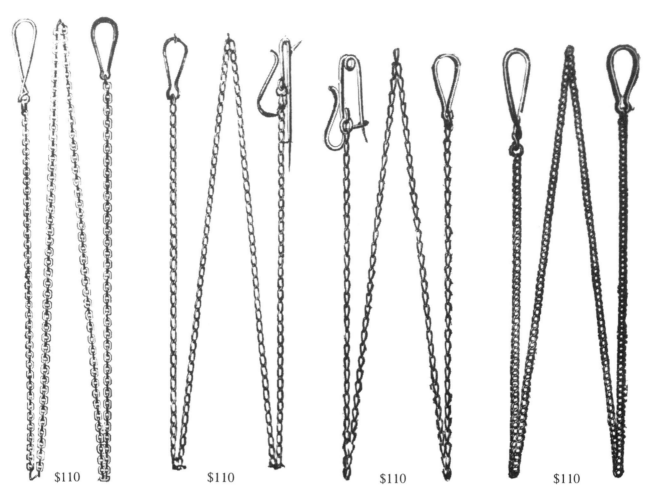

$110 $110 $110 $110

Eyeglass chains, rolled gold plate, circa 1885.

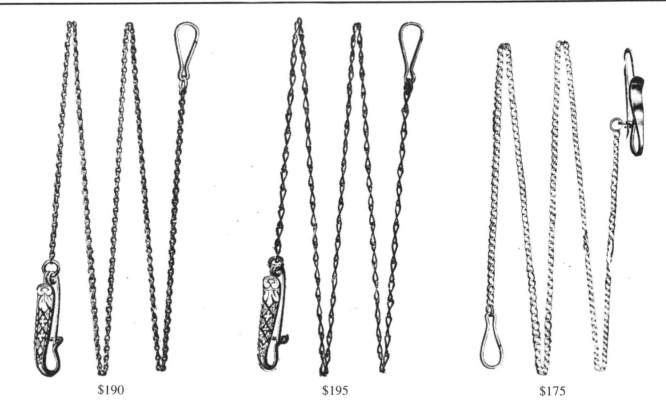

$190 $195 $175

Eyeglass chains, solid gold, circa 1885.

54

10k chain,
14k charm
$230

10k chain,
14k charm
$255

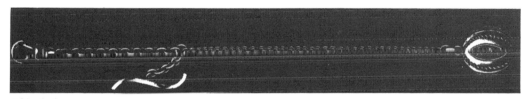

10k chain,
14k charm
$230

10k chain,
14k charm
$230

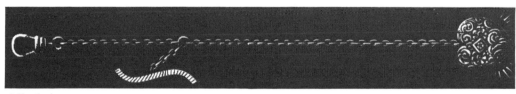

14k chain,
14k charm, diamond
$300

14k chain,
14k charm
$300

Victoria chains, circa 1896.

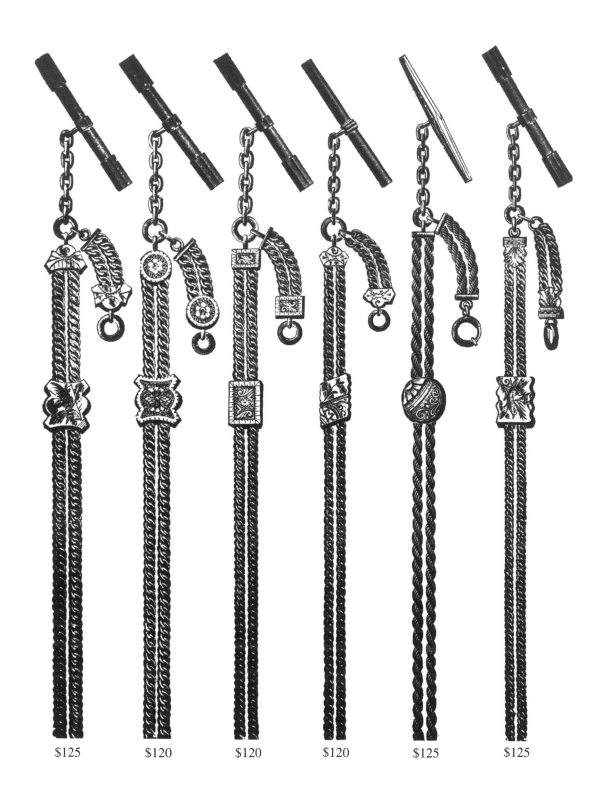

$125 $120 $120 $120 $125 $125

Vest chains, all in rolled gold plate,
circa 1896.

$120 $125 $130

Pony vest chains, circa 1896, all rolled gold
plate with sardonic fobs.

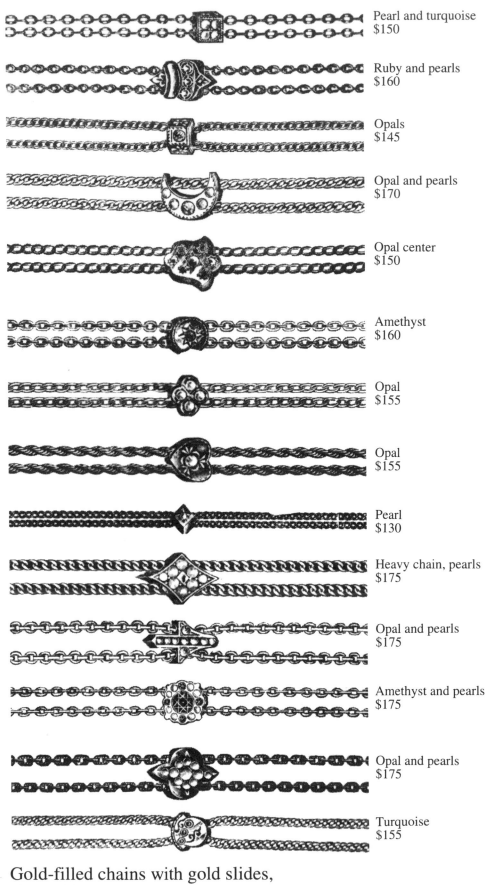

Pearl and turquoise
$150

Ruby and pearls
$160

Opals
$145

Opal and pearls
$170

Opal center
$150

Amethyst
$160

Opal
$155

Opal
$155

Pearl
$130

Heavy chain, pearls
$175

Opal and pearls
$175

Amethyst and pearls
$175

Opal and pearls
$175

Turquoise
$155

Gold-filled chains with gold slides,
circa 1902.

Pink and yellow
gold-filled,
seven jewel
Rima movement
$125

Yellow 10k rolled
gold plate,
seven jewel
Schwob movement
$120

Cloisonne,
yellow rolled
gold plate
Schwob movement
$110

Gold-filled,
seven jewel
Rima movement
$125

Pink and yellow
gold-filled,
seven jewel Rima
movement
$135

Pink and yellow
gold-filled,
seven jewel Rima
movement
$125

Pink and yellow
gold-filled,
seven jewel Rima
movement
$125

Yellow 10k rolled
gold plate,
seven jewel
Schwob movement
$120

Yellow 10k rolled
gold plate and
Lucite, seven
jewel Schwob
movement
$120

Yellow 10k
rolled gold
plate, seven
jewel Schwob
movement
$100

Yellow gold
filled,
seven jewel
Rima movement
$105

Fob watches, circa 1943.

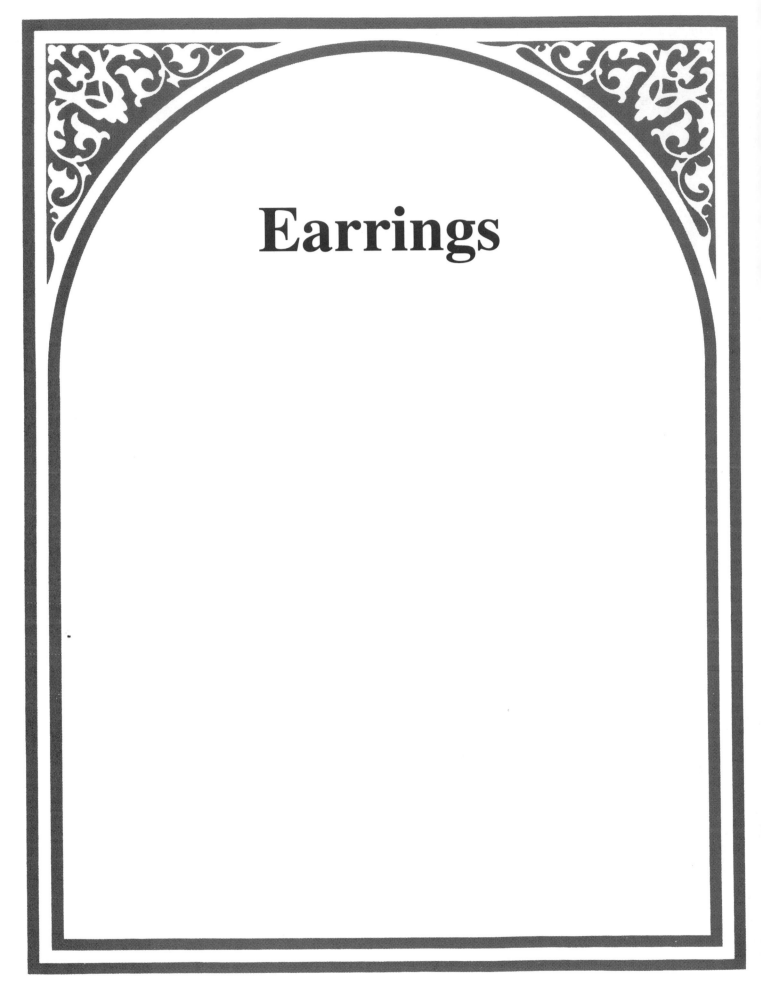

Earrings

Black enamel,
1880-1890
$140

Seed pearls,
1880-1890
$140

Imitation garnet,
seed pearls,
1890-1900
$200

Coral,
1870-1880
$200

Earrings with low karat gold mountings, priced
as pairs.

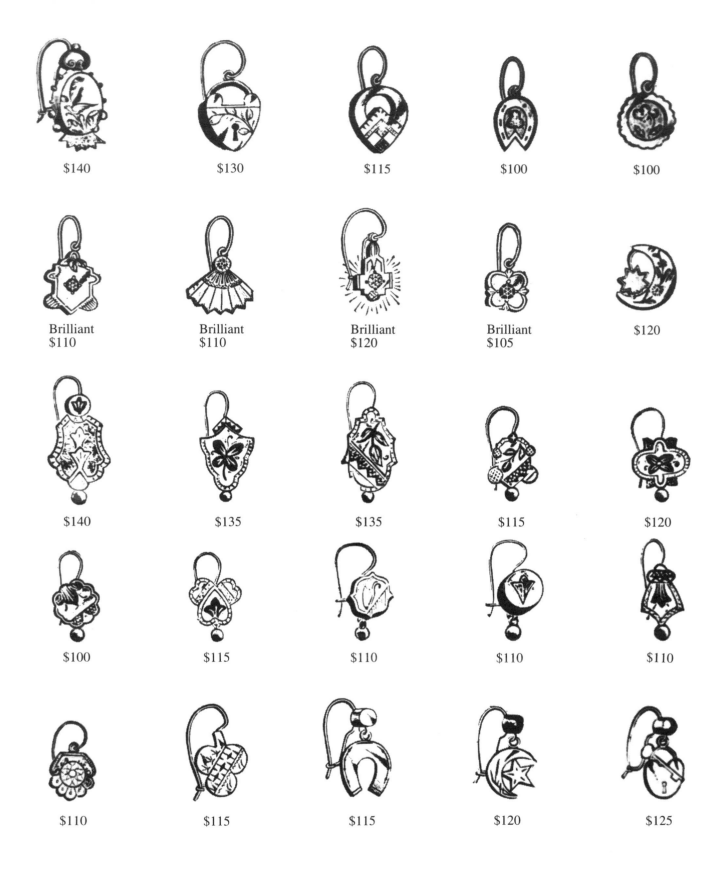

$140	$130	$115	$100	$100
Brilliant $110	Brilliant $110	Brilliant $120	Brilliant $105	$120
$140	$135	$135	$115	$120
$100	$115	$110	$110	$110
$110	$115	$115	$120	$125

Earrings with gold fronts, circa 1880-1890.
These and all other earrings in this book are
priced by the pair.

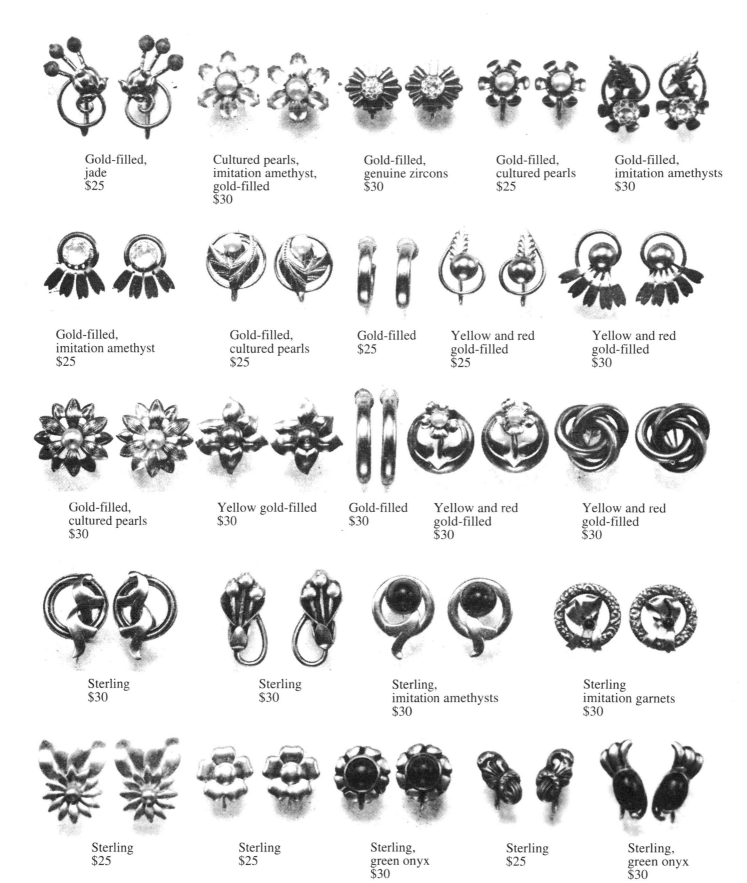

Gold-filled,
jade
$25

Cultured pearls,
imitation amethyst,
gold-filled
$30

Gold-filled,
genuine zircons
$30

Gold-filled,
cultured pearls
$25

Gold-filled,
imitation amethysts
$30

Gold-filled,
imitation amethyst
$25

Gold-filled,
cultured pearls
$25

Gold-filled
$25

Yellow and red
gold-filled
$25

Yellow and red
gold-filled
$30

Gold-filled,
cultured pearls
$30

Yellow gold-filled
$30

Gold-filled
$30

Yellow and red
gold-filled
$30

Yellow and red
gold-filled
$30

Sterling
$30

Sterling
$30

Sterling,
imitation amethysts
$30

Sterling
imitation garnets
$30

Sterling
$25

Sterling
$25

Sterling,
green onyx
$30

Sterling
$25

Sterling,
green onyx
$30

Earrings, circa 1943.

Fobs and
Emblem Charms

Gold-filled,
1900-1910
$60

1910-1920
$55

1910-1920
$55

Fobs pictured date from the early twentieth
century. All except fob at top are gold plated.

1910-1920
$55

1910-1920
$55

$110	$110	$110	$110	$110
$120	$120	$90	$125	$125
$125	$120	$120	$120	$120
$110	$110	$110	$110	$110

Solid gold charms, circa 1896.

66

$45 $45 $50 $50 $50

$50 $50 $50 $45 $50

$50 $50 $55 $50 $50

$50 $55 $55 $55 $50

Charms, circa 1896, all in rolled gold plate.

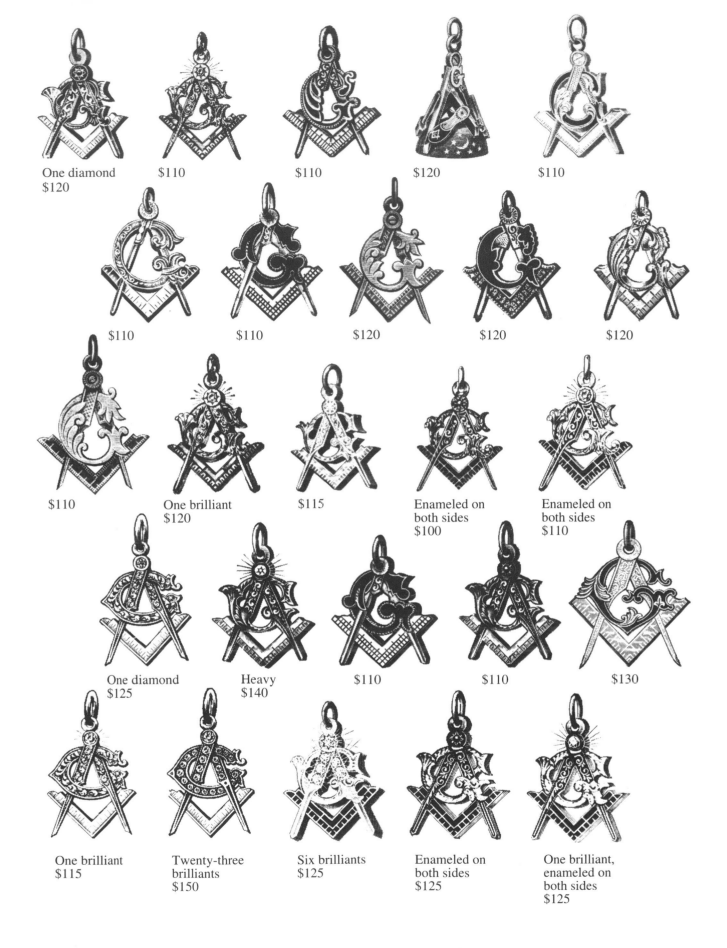

One diamond
$120

$110

$110

$120

$110

$110

$110

$120

$120

$120

$110

One brilliant
$120

$115

Enameled on
both sides
$100

Enameled on
both sides
$110

One diamond
$125

Heavy
$140

$110

$110

$130

One brilliant
$115

Twenty-three
brilliants
$150

Six brilliants
$125

Enameled on
both sides
$125

One brilliant,
enameled on
both sides
$125

Solid gold charms, circa 1917.

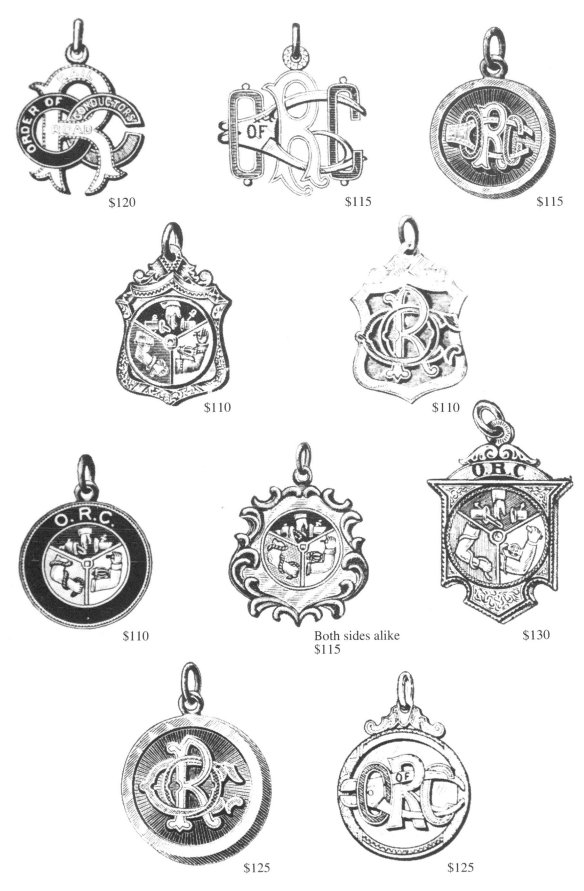

$120

$115

$115

$110

$110

$110

Both sides alike
$115

$130

$125

$125

Emblem charms, Order of Railroad Conductors, circa 1917, solid gold.

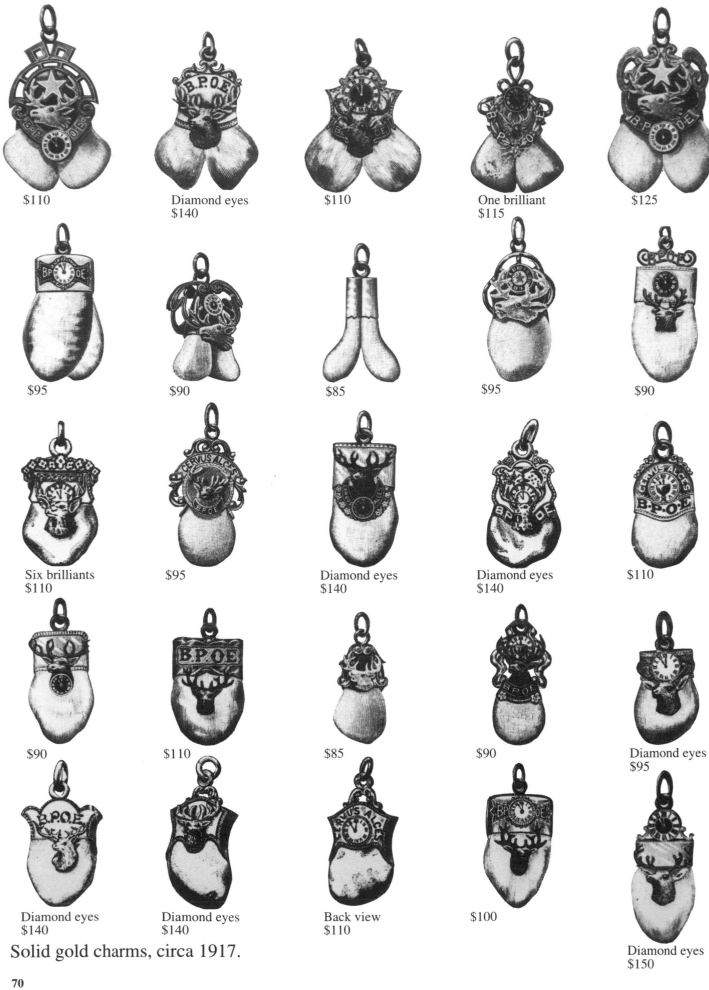

$110

Diamond eyes
$140

$110

One brilliant
$115

$125

$95

$90

$85

$95

$90

Six brilliants
$110

$95

Diamond eyes
$140

Diamond eyes
$140

$110

$90

$110

$85

$90

Diamond eyes
$95

Diamond eyes
$140

Diamond eyes
$140

Back view
$110

$100

Diamond eyes
$150

Solid gold charms, circa 1917.

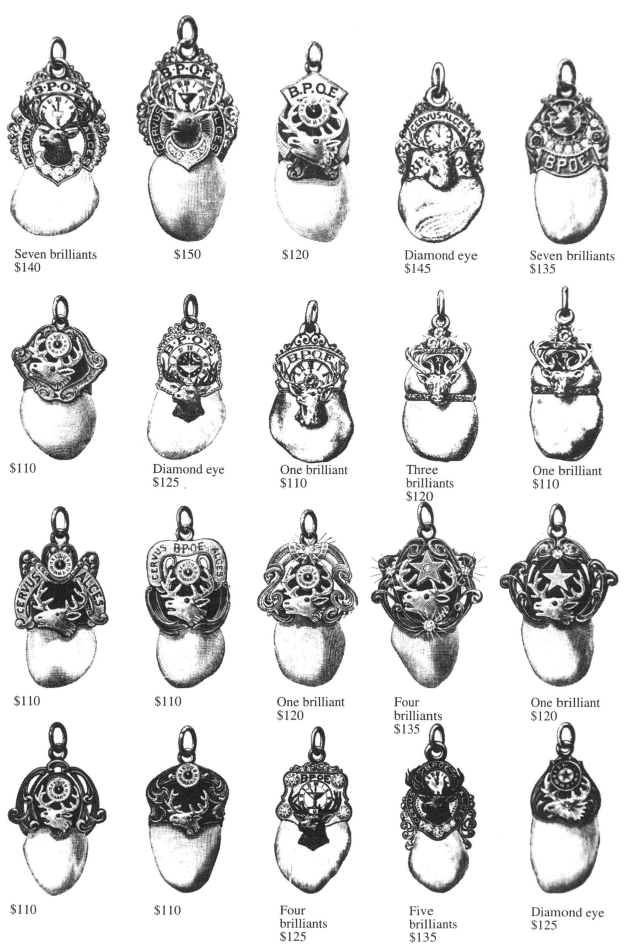

Seven brilliants
$140

$150

$120

Diamond eye
$145

Seven brilliants
$135

$110

Diamond eye
$125

One brilliant
$110

Three
brilliants
$120

One brilliant
$110

$110

$110

One brilliant
$120

Four
brilliants
$135

One brilliant
$120

$110

$110

Four
brilliants
$125

Five
brilliants
$135

Diamond eye
$125

Solid gold charms, circa 1917.

$85 $80 $80 $100 $100

$60 $60 $60 $80 $80

$80 $80 $80 $80 $80

$90 $90 $90 $90 $80

$80 $80 $80 $85 $90

Solid gold fraternal charms, circa 1917.

(Top to bottom) Stone cameo brooch, gold front, circa 1860, $400. Stone cameo brooch, gold front, circa 1856, $450. Stone cameo brooch, gold front, circa 1860, $275. Stone cameo brooch, gold front, circa 1860, $250.

(Top to bottom) Child's gold-filled locket, circa 1905, $85. Yellow 10k gold locket with diamond, circa 1930, $225. Gold-filled locket, circa 1910, $110. Gold-filled moon and star locket with brilliants, circa 1910, $110. Larger gold-filled moon and star locket with brilliants, circa 1910, $140.

(Top to bottom) Bracelet with sterling silver top, circa 1915-1930, $125. Pendant, carved ivory nude, sterling silver, circa 1915, $200. Necklace, 14k gold with platinum overlay, crystal and diamond center, circa 1925, $325.

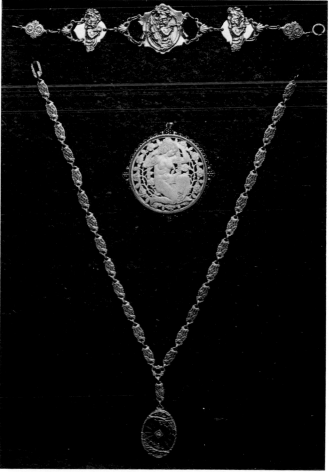

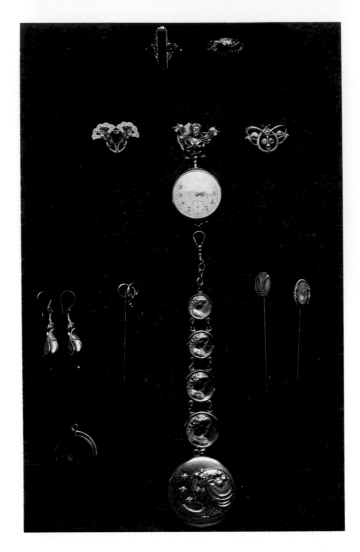

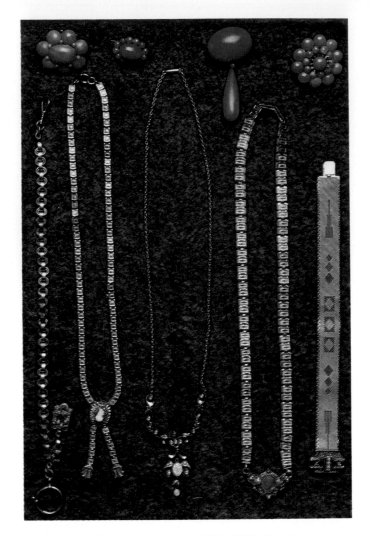

(Row 1, L to R) Ring, banded agate set in white gold, circa 1880, $425. Garnet ring, gold mounting, circa 1880, $425.

(Row 2) Watch pin, 14k gold, three sapphires, one pearl, circa 1900, $225. Watch pin and watch, circa 1900; watch pin, 10k gold, $200; watch, 14k gold, $275. Watch pin, inlaid 10k gold with seed pearls, circa 1900, $200.

(Row 3) Gold-filled earrings, circa 1915, $65. Stickpin, gold-filled, circa 1910, $35. Watch chain with locket, both 14k gold, five rose-cut diamonds, circa 1910, $675. Gold-filled stickpin, circa 1910, $35. Gold-filled stickpin, coral setting, circa 1910, $65.

(Row 4) Gold-filled fob, intaglio setting, circa 1910, $75.

(Row 1, L to R) Coral pin, circa 1880, $175. Coral pin, circa 1880, $175. Coral pin with teardrop, circa 1880, $200. Coral pin, circa 1880, $175.

(Row 2) Gold watch chain, circa 1890 $625. Gold-filled cameo necklace, circa 1865-1880, $350. Gold necklace, set with opals, rubies, and pearls, circa 1865-1880, $675. Gold-filled necklace with coral cameo, circa 1865-1880, $400. Bracelet, 14k gold set with pearls, circa 1865-1880, $550.

(Row 1, L to R) Gold-filled earrings, circa 1880, $150. Gold-filled earrings, circa 1880, $150

(Row 2) Gold-filled pin with mosaic set in goldstone, circa 1880, $250. Locket 14k gold, circa 1880, $350.

(Row 3) Gold-filled pin, circa 1880, $110. Pin, 14k gold, circa 1880, $225.

(Row 4) Watch 14k rose gold with cameo slide, circa 1890, $600. Sardonic fob with intaglio setting, circa 1895, $125. Gold-filled necklace, circa 1880, $250. Gold fob, circa 1895, $125. Enameled watch with seed pearls, circa 1880, $375.

(Row 1, L to R) Ring, sterling with marcasites and black onyx, $125. Ring, 14k white gold, onyx with crystal diamond chip, $150. Ring, sterling with marcasites and green onyx, $125. Ring, sterling with marcasites and synthetic amethyst, $125. Ring, 14k gold with rubies and diamonds, $450.

(Row 2) Necklace, 14k gold, circa 1935, $200. Pendant-brooch, 14k gold with diamonds and sapphires, circa 1930, $225. Necklace-watch, 10k gold with diamond, black enamel, Swiss movement, circa 1930, $350. Sterling earrings with marcasites and onyx, circa 1935, $90. Necklace, 14k gold with diamond, circa 1935, $250.

(Row 3) Bracelet, 14k white gold, circa 1935, $450.

(Row 4) Bracelet, 14k white gold, circa 1935, $425.

(Row 1, L to R) Lorgnette, 14k gold, circa 1890, $900. Eyeglass case, 14k gold, alligator skin, circa 1900, $2,200. Money clip, 14k gold, ruby eye, circa 1905, $490.

(Row 2) Mesh pocketbook, 18k gold, circa 1905, $1,800. Watch chain, human hair, circa 1890, $225. Handkerchief holder, 14k gold, circa 1890, $390.

(*Row 1, Top to Bottom*) Gold watch pin, circa 1900, $185. Gold locket, circa 1870-1890, $425. Gold earrings, circa 1880, $275. Gold brooch with turquoise stones, circa 1880, $225. Gold-filled brooch, banded agate, circa 1860-1890, $225.

(*Row 2*) Gold necklace, black onyx, gold overlay, circa 1870-1890, $3,000. Gold swivel watch clip, circa 1880, $1,100.

(*Row 3*) Gold sardonic shell cameo brooch, circa 1860-1880, $375. Silver brooch, sardonic shell cameo, circa 1860-1880, $275. Gold cornilian shell cameo brooch, circa 1880-1900, $325. Painted porcelain brooch, sterling mounting, circa 1895, $200. Cornilian shell cameo brooch, gold-filled mounting, circa 1875, $325.

(Row 1, L to R) Slide chain, 14k gold, circa 1870-1890, $450. Slide chain and gold-filled locket with sardonic inlay, $325. Bracelet, turquoise and seed pearls, gold mounting, circa 1880-1900, $500. Bracelet, turquoise and seed pearls, gold mounting, circa 1880-1890, $500.

(Row 2, Top to Bottom) Man's gold Elgin watch and chain, gold fob with bloodstone intaglio, circa 1890-1900, $900. Brooch, gold-filled, human hair, circa 1870-1890, $250. Earrings, gold-filled, circa 1870-1890, $150.

(Row 1, L to R) Ring, garnet set in gold, $250. Ring, garnet and seed pearls in gold, $375. Ring, garnets and seed pearls in gold, $400. Ring, garnet set in gold, $295.

(Row 2) Earrings, garnets, gold-filled, $195. Necklace, garnets, gilded silver, $700. Stickpin, garnets, gold-filled, $115.

(Row 3) Brooch, garnets set in gilded silver, $200. Fan-shaped brooch, garnets set in gilded silver, $225.

(Row 4) Bracelet, garnets set in brass, $485. All Victorian jewelry pictured above, circa 1880-1890.

(Row 1) Lady's watch, rose-cut diamonds, red and green enameled 18k gold, circa 1895-1915, $1,600.

(Row 2, L to R) Watch and slide, 14k gold, gold-filled chain, circa 1890-1910, $600. Watch, 14k gold, circa 1890-1910, $600. Watch and chain, 14k gold watch, 10k gold chain, circa 1890-1910, $575.

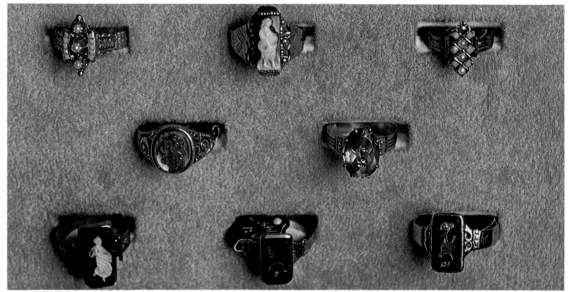

(Row 1, L to R) Ring, turquoise and seed pearls, 14k gold, $325. Ring, onyx, cameo, $390. Ring, turquoise and seed pearls, 10k gold, $300.

(Row 2) Ring, tiger eye, intaglio, $340. Ring, tiny rose-cut diamond, amethyst, gold inlay, 14k gold, $450.

(Row 3) Ring, cameo and seed pearls, 10k gold, $400. Ring, sardonic, rose-cut diamond, 10k gold, $385. Ring, two rose-cut diamonds, black onyx with gold inlay, 10k gold, $385. All rings pictured above, circa 1870-1890.

Genuine elk tooth $115   Genuine elk tooth $100   Genuine elk tooth $110   Genuine elk tooth $95   Genuine elk tooth $100

Genuine elk tooth $110   Genuine elk tooth $110   Genuine elk tooth $110   Genuine elk tooth $110   Genuine elk tooth $110

Genuine elk tooth $110   Genuine elk tooth $110   Genuine elk tooth $95   Genuine elk tooth $95   Genuine elk tooth $100

Genuine elk tooth $100   Genuine elk tooth $110 $85 $85 $85

$85 $85 $85 $85 $85

Solid gold B.P.O.E. charms, circa 1917.

Garnet Jewelry

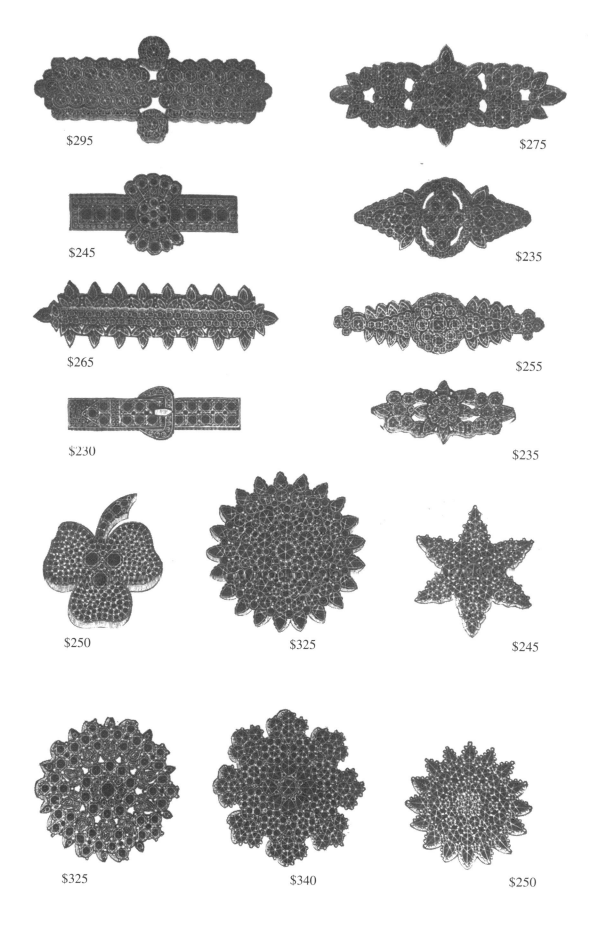

$295

$275

$245

$235

$265

$255

$230

$235

$250

$325

$245

$325

$340

$250

Bohemian garnet brooches with gold mountings, circa 1889.

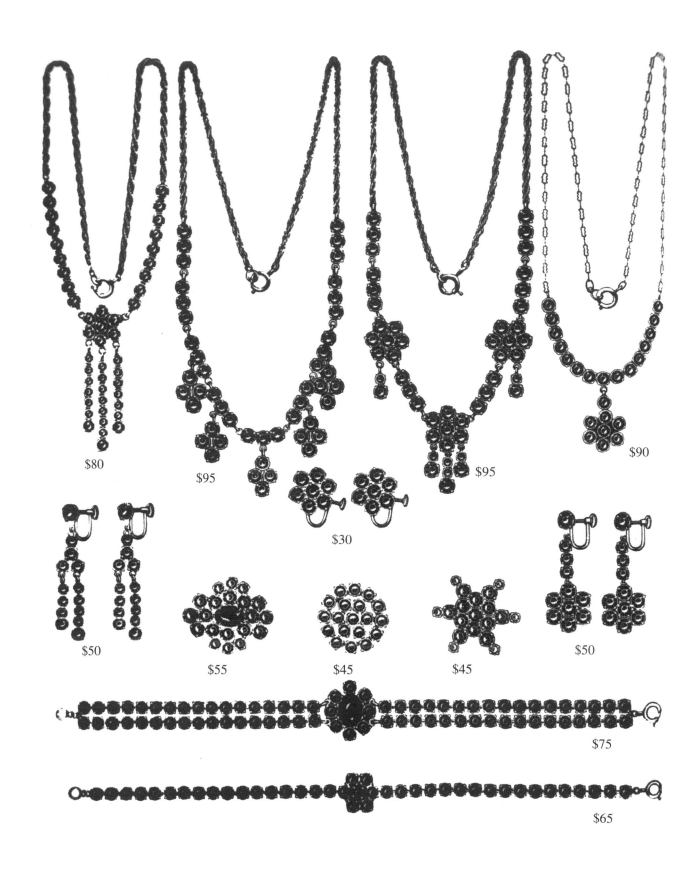

$80

$95

$30

$95

$90

$50

$55

$45

$45

$50

$75

$65

Imitation garnet jewelry in gold plated settings,
circa 1932.

Lavaliers, Lockets, Necklaces, and Pendants

$375 $325

Victorian gold-filled cameo necklaces,
circa 1870-1890.

86

1870-1885
$175

1870-1880
$150

1890-1900
$190

Pendant,
coral,
1865-1875
$175

Gold plated lockets and pendant,
dating from 1865 to 1900.

Circa 1940
imitation diamond
$110

Circa 1930
cornilian cameo
$150

Circa 1930
gold-filled
$125

Gold-filled lockets from the 1930s and 1940s.

$110

$120

$120

Gold-filled lockets, circa 1900-1915;
stones are brilliants.

Imitation topaz
$110

Pale blue enameled locket
$125

Imitation amethyst
$125

Sterling silver necklaces, circa 1930-1940.
Top and bottom necklaces are rhodium-
plated to prevent tarnishing.

Mine cut diamonds,
1870-1880
$325

Onyx,
1890-1900
$200

Black enameling,
1870-1880
$200

Modern spring ring
Victorian period,
seed pearls
$300

Opal,
1890-1900
$300

Lockets with low karat gold mountings.

Painted porcelain front, back,
1890-1900
$275

1895-1910
$325

Pendant
post-1925
Limoges porcelain
$110

Painted porcelain lockets and pendant
with low karat gold mountings.

92

$75

Ruby,
white stones
$80

$75

$75

Ruby, sapphire,
white stone
$85

$70

$70

$75

Enameled
$75

$70

$70

$75

White stone
$75

White stones
$75

White stones
$75

White stone
$75

Ruby,
white stone
$85

White stone
$85

$70

$70

White stones
$75

$70

$70

Emerald and
white stones
$80

Emerald and
white stones
$80

Gold-filled fob type lockets, circa 1896.

Turquoise
$165

$165

Turquoise
$190

Brilliants
$175

Brilliants
$175

$160

Brilliants
$200

$175

$175

Gold-filled Art Nouveau lockets, circa 1907.

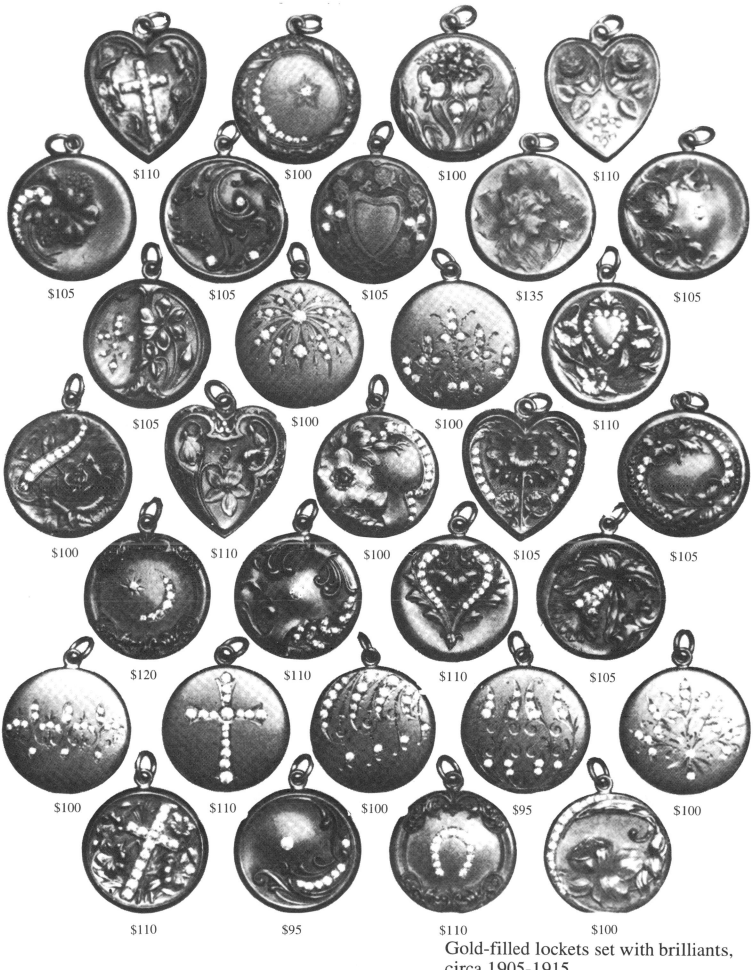

$110 $100 $100 $110

$105 $105 $105 $135 $105

$105 $100 $100 $110

$100 $110 $100 $105 $105

$120 $110 $110 $105

$100 $110 $100 $95 $100

$110 $95 $110 $100

Gold-filled lockets set with brilliants, circa 1905-1915.

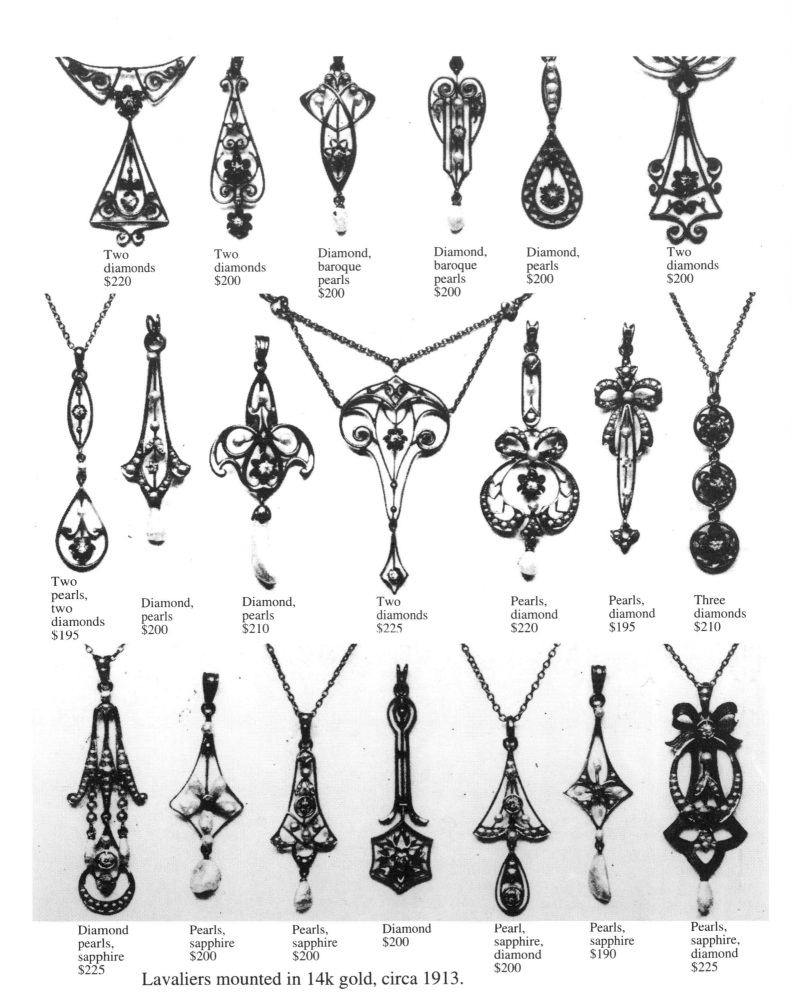

Two
diamonds
$220

Two
diamonds
$200

Diamond,
baroque
pearls
$200

Diamond,
baroque
pearls
$200

Diamond,
pearls
$200

Two
diamonds
$200

Two
pearls,
two
diamonds
$195

Diamond,
pearls
$200

Diamond,
pearls
$210

Two
diamonds
$225

Pearls,
diamond
$220

Pearls,
diamond
$195

Three
diamonds
$210

Diamond
pearls,
sapphire
$225

Pearls,
sapphire
$200

Pearls,
sapphire
$200

Diamond
$200

Pearl,
sapphire,
diamond
$200

Pearls,
sapphire
$190

Pearls,
sapphire,
diamond
$225

Lavaliers mounted in 14k gold, circa 1913.

Sapphires, pearls
$185

Diamond, two
sapphires, and pearls
$185

Diamond, sapphire,
and pearls
$185

Sapphire,
baroque pearl
$175

Diamond,
baroque pearls
$185

Diamond
$175

Diamond,
baroque pearl
$185

Diamond, pearls
$250

Imitation amethyst,
baroque pearls
$185

Gold filigree,
amethyst bands
$195

Gold filigree
$180

Sapphire, diamond, and
pearls
$190

Diamond,
amethysts, pearls
$190

Diamond,
baroque pearls,
and pearls
$190

Sapphire and pearls
$185

Imitation amethyst,
baroque pearl
$185

Lavaliers mounted in 10k gold, circa 1913.

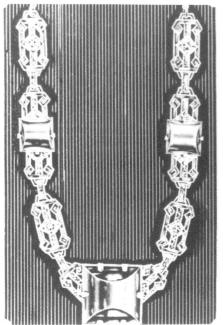

Sterling,
marcasites,
and chrysoprase
$130

Sterling,
marcasites
$130

Sterling
marcasites
$130

Sterling,
marcasites,
and chrysoprase
$130

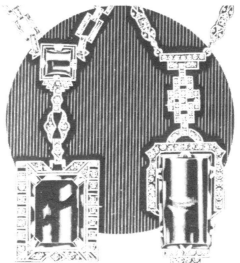

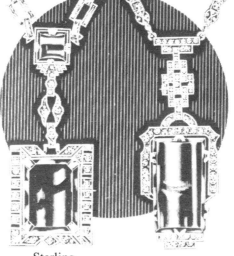

Sterling,
marcasites,
and black onyx
$130

Sterling,
marcasites,
and black
onyx
$155

Sterling,
marcasites,
and black onyx
$155

Sterling,
marcasites,
and black onyx
$155

Rhodium,
marcasites,
and
imitation
emerald
$115

Sterling,
marcasites,
and
imitation
amethyst
$115

Rhodium,
marcasites,
imitation
pearls, and crystals
$115

Sterling,
marcasites,
and imitation
emerald
$115

Necklaces mounted in sterling or rhodium, circa 1932.

Chrome finish
green onyx
$100

Sterling,
imitation
onyx and
brilliants
$110

Chrome finish,
imitation jet
$100

Rhodium,
marcasite,
and pearl
$100

Green and red
gold-filled,
turquoise
$100

Sterling,
frosted crystal,
brilliant
$110

Sterling,
amethyst
$110

Rhodium,
imitation blue
sapphire,
brilliant
$100

Chrome finish,
imitation
zircon
$95

Sterling,
amethyst
$100

Assorted necklaces, circa 1932.

Sterling,
onyx, imitation
crystal,
brilliant
$120

Rhodium,
imitation
crystal,
brilliant
$95

Rhodium,
black onyx,
brilliant,
crystal
$95

Chrome finish
imitation
emerald
$95

Sterling,
brilliant,
imitation
onyx
$110

Rhodium,
brilliant,
imitation
black onyx
$120

Yellow gold-filled,
green stones
$120

White 14k
gold-filled,
one brilliant,
two emeralds
$120

Rhodium,
one brilliant
$120

Sterling,
cornilian
shell cameo
$150

Assorted necklaces, circa 1932.

Green 14k
gold,
six genuine
zircons
$200

Yellow 14k
gold,
six diamonds
$220

Yellow 14k
gold,
two genuine
garnets
$200

Yellow 14k
gold,
genuine
zircon
$200

Yellow 14k
gold,
genuine
zircon and
four
diamonds
$200

White 14k
gold,
one diamond
in crystal
$225

Yellow 14k
gold, with
genuine jade
$200

Yellow 14k
gold, with
one diamond
$195

Yellow 10k
gold, blue
green zircon,
and two
diamonds
$185

Yellow 10k
gold,
one diamond
$200

Yellow 10k
gold with
genuine
zircon
$190

Green 14k
gold, jade
$200

Yellow 10k
gold, one
diamond,
cornilian
cameo
$225

Yellow 10k
gold, black
onyx, and
one diamond
$185

Yellow 10k
gold, one
diamond
$180

Yellow 10k
gold,
genuine
zircon
$185

Yellow 10k
gold, one
diamond,
black onyx
$185

Yellow 10k
gold with
cornilian
cameo
$225

Assorted necklaces, circa 1940.

1/20 12k
$85

1/10 14k
$85

1/20 10k
one diamond
$80

1/10 14k
$85

1/20 10k
$80

1/20 10k,
cornilian
cameo
$125

1/20 12k
$85

1/20 10k,
four
photographs
$75

1/20 12k
$85

1/20 10k
$90

1/20 10k
$80

1/20 12k,
cornilian
cameo
$100

1/20 10k
$85

1/20 10k
$75

1/20 12k
$85

1/20 12k
$75

1/20 10k
imitation
turquoise
and pearls
$80

1/20 12k
$80

1/20 12k
$80

Yellow gold-filled lockets, circa 1940. All except
one are designed to hold two photographs.

102

Black enamel
inlay
$60

Engine turned
$55

Black enamel
inlay, four
pictures
$60

Black enamel
inlay, four
pictures
$50

Applied cross,
four pictures
$50

Cornilian
cameo
$135

Cornilian
cameo
$125

Cornilian
cameo
$100

Black onyx,
one fine
diamond
$90

Black and white
enamel
$60

One fine
diamond
$75

Roman finish,
one fine
diamond
$75

Engraved,
one fine
diamond
$80

Engraved,
one fine
diamond
$75

Engraved,
one fine
diamond
$90

One fine
diamond
$70

One fine
diamond
$70

One fine
diamond
$85

Imitation
amethysts
$75

Imitation
garnets
$75

Gold-filled lockets, circa 1941. All will hold two
pictures, except three in top row.

Bright
finish
$150

Bright
finish
$125

Black onyx,
one diamond
$155

Embossed,
engraved
$140

Embossed,
engraved
$155

Bright
finish
$155

Bright
finish
$115

Roman
finish
$135

Roman
finish
$135

Roman
finish
$135

Bright
finish
$155

Roman
finish
$170

Engraved
$80

Engraved
$70

Engraved
$65

Embossed,
engraved
$80

Embossed,
engraved
$85

Cornilian
cameo
$100

Engine
turned
$55

Black onyx
$65

Cornilian
cameo
$75

Black
enamel
$60

Engine
turned
$45

Engraved
$45

Two-picture lockets, circa 1941. Top two rows
are all 10k yellow gold. Last two lockets in bottom
row are sterling silver; remainder are gold-filled.

Miscellaneous

$175 $185 $185

$160 $150 $170 $130

$215 $265 $375 $395

Selection of gold crosses, circa 1880-1890. Top and center rows: rolled gold plate. Bottom row examples are all solid gold.

Mourning Jewelry

Carved jet brooch
$180

Carved jet earrings
$190

French jet (black glass)
cameo brooch
$275

Mourning brooch,
gold, black enamel, hair
$300

Mourning brooch,
gilt, black enamel, hair
$300

Jet jewelry, circa 1850-1880.

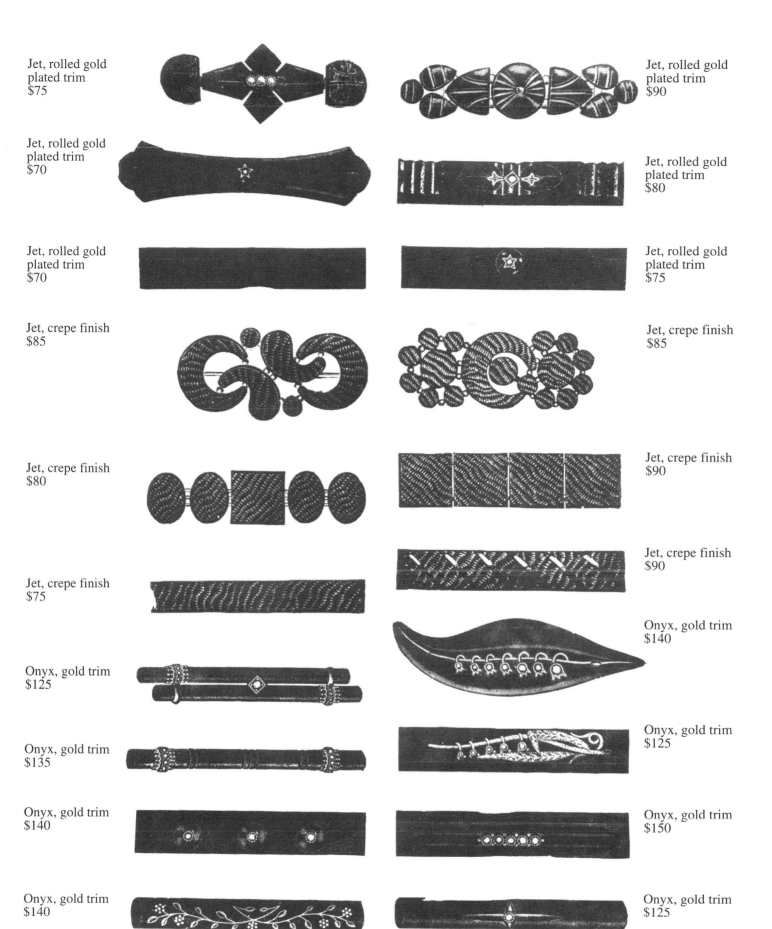

Jet, rolled gold plated trim $75

Jet, rolled gold plated trim $90

Jet, rolled gold plated trim $70

Jet, rolled gold plated trim $80

Jet, rolled gold plated trim $70

Jet, rolled gold plated trim $75

Jet, crepe finish $85

Jet, crepe finish $85

Jet, crepe finish $80

Jet, crepe finish $90

Jet, crepe finish $75

Jet, crepe finish $90

Onyx, gold trim $140

Onyx, gold trim $125

Onyx, gold trim $125

Onyx, gold trim $135

Onyx, gold trim $140

Onyx, gold trim $150

Onyx, gold trim $140

Onyx, gold trim $125

Selection of bar pins, circa 1889.

Pendant
$225

Locket
$250

Locket
$275

Locket
$300

Carved jet pendant and lockets, circa 1860-1880.

French jet,
cut and polished,
gilt scroll,
plaited hair
$200

Carved bog oak
$300

Dark tortoiseshell,
gold and silver initials,
hair
$200

French jet,
gold frame,
plaited hair
$200

Carved bog oak
$350

Gilt and black enamel,
hair
$250

Brooches and crosses, circa 1850-1870.

Rings

White 18k gold
with diamonds
$2,000

White 14k gold
with diamonds
$1,800

Platinum and
diamonds
$5,500

Pink 10k gold
with six synthetic
rubies
$275

Pink 10k gold
with four
synthetic rubies
$275

Pink 10k gold,
synthetic rubies
$275

Yellow 10k gold,
genuine opal,
six synthetic rubies
$290

Pink 10k gold
with three synthetic
rubies, three pearls
$250

Pink 10k gold,
genuine rubies
and diamonds
$500

Rings, circa 1930-1940

Opals, garnets and pearls $140	Artificial oriental pearls $125	Emerald and twenty pearls $200	Opals, emeralds, and pearls $150	Three opals, eight pearls $125

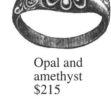

Artificial pink pearls $125	Pearls, emeralds, and rubies $200	Opals, pearls, amethysts $160	Two rubies, three opals $140	Three garnets, two pearls $140

Opal $130	Opal $130	One ruby, twenty-four pearls $145	Opal and amethyst $215	Garnet $155

Ruby $130	Three opals, six pearls $125	Two rubies, five pearls $135	Four opals, nine pearls $135	Emeralds, rubies, pearls $140

Three rubies, six pearls $160	Turquoise, pearls $125	Three amethysts, six pearls $155	Two opals, three rubies, twelve pearls $150	Opal, six rubies $170

Two rubies $145	Ruby, pearls $160	Pearl, amethyst $150	Artificial pearls $125	Opal, twelve pearls $200

Opal $150	Opal, two rubies $150	Three opals $145	Bloodstone $125	Opal $150

Ladies' solid gold rings, circa 1900-1910.

Green 10k gold
$215

White 10k gold
$145

Green 14k gold
$225

Green 10k gold
$195

Green 10k gold
$125

White 18k gold,
black onyx,
one diamond
$225

White 18k gold,
black onyx,
one diamond
$185

White 14k gold,
one diamond
$180

White 18k gold,
black onyx
$200

Green 10k gold
$125

White 14k gold,
black onyx,
one diamond
$285

White 10k gold,
six diamonds
$225

White 10k gold,
six diamonds,
onyx
$275

Yellow 10k gold,
six diamonds,
black onyx
$265

White 10k gold,
six diamonds,
black onyx
$265

White 14k gold,
black onyx
$210

Green 14k gold,
black onyx
$195

White 10k gold,
one diamond,
black onyx
$185

Green 10k gold,
black onyx
$210

White 10k gold,
black onyx
$195

Men's rings, circa 1932.

Marcasites,
hematite
$105

Marcasites,
hematite
$95

Marcasites,
crystal
$95

Marcasites,
black onyx
$95

Marcasites,
black onyx
$85

Marcasites,
black onyx
$95

Marcasites,
black onyx
$95

Marcasites,
black onyx
$115

Marcasites,
black onyx
$75

Marcasites,
black onyx
$90

Reversible,
green
synthetic
zircon,
onyx,
one diamond
$190

Reversible,
onyx,
cornilian
cameo
$240

Reversible,
onyx,
diamond,
cameo
$225

Onyx,
diamond,
cameo,
diamond
$240

Reversible,
cameo,
diamond,
crystal
$310

Reversible,
onyx,
diamond,
crystal
$300

Cameo,
crystal,
diamond
$210

Ruby,
diamond,
crystal,
diamond
$255

Onyx with
diamond,
synthetic ruby
$180

Onyx,
diamond,
genuine
amethyst
$210

Onyx with
diamond,
cameo
$200

Cameo,
diamond,
onyx
$290

Cameo,
diamond,
four
aquamarines
$300

Ladies' rings, circa 1932. Top two rows have
sterling silver mountings. Four necklaces and
remainder of rings are mounted in 14k white gold.

116

Aquamarine
$210

Deep amethyst
$210

Aquamarine
$210

Amethyst
$220

Synthetic
emerald
$170

Amethyst
$210

Topaz
$180

Brilliant black
opal
$180

One diamond,
black onyx
$210

Two diamonds
aquamarine
$240

One diamond,
four aquamarines
$240

Black onyx,
one diamond
$220

Two diamonds,
aquamarine
$230

Two diamonds,
aquamarine
$240

Two diamonds,
aquamarine
$240

Two diamonds,
aquamarine
$240

Black onyx,
one diamond
$200

Black onyx,
one diamond
$200

Black onyx,
two diamonds
$210

Black onyx,
one diamond
$240

Men's fraternal rings, circa 1932, mounted in 14k white gold.

14k, diamond
$220

14k, diamond
$220

Diamond
$210

14k
$200

14k, diamond
$235

Diamond
$210

Black onyx,
two diamonds
$210

14k
$185

Diamond
$200

Synthetic
sapphire
$185

Black onyx
$195

Black onyx
$195

$190

Synthetic
blue spinel
$180

Black onyx
$185

Black onyx
$200

Diamond,
ruby eyes
$200

14k
$200

14k
$200

Black enamel
$200

Black onyx
$180

14k,
one diamond,
five synthetic
stones
$175

Black onyx
$175

Enameling
$175

Black onyx
$175

Men's fraternal rings, circa 1940. Most are
mounted in 10k yellow gold. Seven have 14k
yellow gold mountings and are so identified.

14k,
black onyx,
one diamond
$200

14k,
black onyx
three diamonds
$200

14k,
black onyx,
seven diamonds
$250

14k,
black onyx,
five diamonds
$220

14k,
black onyx
one diamond
$190

Black onyx,
one diamond
$185

Black onyx,
one diamond
$185

Black onyx,
one diamond
$185

Black onyx,
one diamond
$200

Black onyx
$200

14k,
cornilian
cameo
$200

Cornilian
cameo
$200

One diamond,
cornilian
cameo
$215

Opal
$200

Opal
$200

Hematite
intaglio,
two diamonds
$200

Tiger eye cameo
$200

Tiger eye cameo
$200

Hematite
intaglio
$200

Black onyx
intaglio
$200

Ladies' rings, circa 1940, in 10k yellow gold
mountings unless otherwise identified.

Red gold trim,
four synthetic
rubies
$240

Genuine
zircon
$215

Red gold trim,
three
synthetic
rubies
$240

Red,
white gold
trim
$225

Genuine
zircon
$215

Genuine
amethyst
$240

Red,
yellow gold
trim
$200

Red gold trim,
genuine zircon
$215

Genuine
zircon
$215

Red
gold trim
$210

Genuine
amethyst
$225

Red gold
trim,
genuine
zircon
$225

Red
gold trim
$200

Red gold trim,
genuine
zircon
$210

Red gold
trim,
genuine
amethyst
$225

Ladies' rings, circa 1942, all mounted in 14k
yellow gold.

Section II

Baby Jewelry

$110

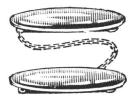

Rolled gold plate
two-piece pin set
$85

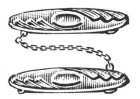

Rolled gold plate
two-piece pin set
$85

10 karat solid gold
pin set
$110

Gold-filled
chain pin set
$100

Gold-filled pin set
$95

Baby pin sets circa 1895.

Gold-filled 1-1/2 inches diameter
$65

Gold-filled 1-1/2 inches diameter
$55

Rolled gold plate bib holder
$45

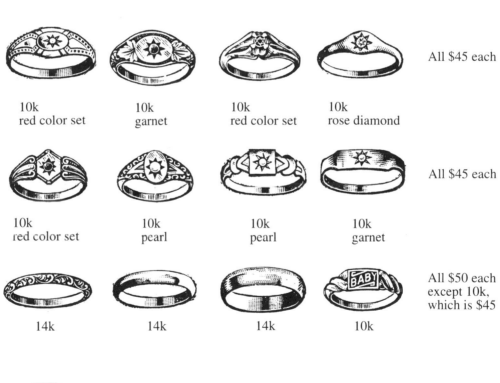

All $45 each

| 10k red color set | 10k garnet | 10k red color set | 10k rose diamond |

All $45 each

| 10k red color set | 10k pearl | 10k pearl | 10k garnet |

All $50 each
except 10k,
which is $45

| 14k | 14k | 14k | 10k |

All $45 each
except 14k,
which is $50

| 10k | 10k | 10k | 14k |

Cameos

These are extra quality shell cameo bracelets mounted in sterling silver
and hand-carved in Italy. The illustrations below are as close as possible
to actual size.

Profiles, $200

Profiles and Flowers, $225

Profiles, $275

The Muses, $400

The Seven Days of the Week, $600

| Sunday | Saturday | Friday | Thursday | Wednesday | Tuesday | Monday |
| Apollo | Saturnus | Venus | Jupiter | Mercury | Mars | Diana |

The Seven Days of the Week, $650

Shell cameo bracelets mounted in sterling silver.
Produced in Italy after 1950.

The Muses, $600

The Seven Days of the Week, $600

Profiles of the Seven Deities of the Week, $400

Profiles, $275

Lava cameo bracelet produced after 1950
(assorted shades of lava)

The Seven Days of the Week, $1,000

Distinguishing Characteristics of Shell Cameos

Shell Cameos are carved on three different types of shells, as follows:

Cornilian Shell: Reddish orange background,
white creamish carved figure.

Rosaline Shell: Light pale pink background,
pure white carved figure.

Sardonic Shell: Dark brown background,
pure white carved figure.

Size: 45mm
unmounted

Size: 45mm
sterling mount

Size: 40mm
unmounted

Size: 45mm
sterling mount

Size: 50mm
sterling mount

Size: 45mm
sterling mount

Examples of shell cameos produced in Italy after 1950.

Eyeglass Chains
and Reels

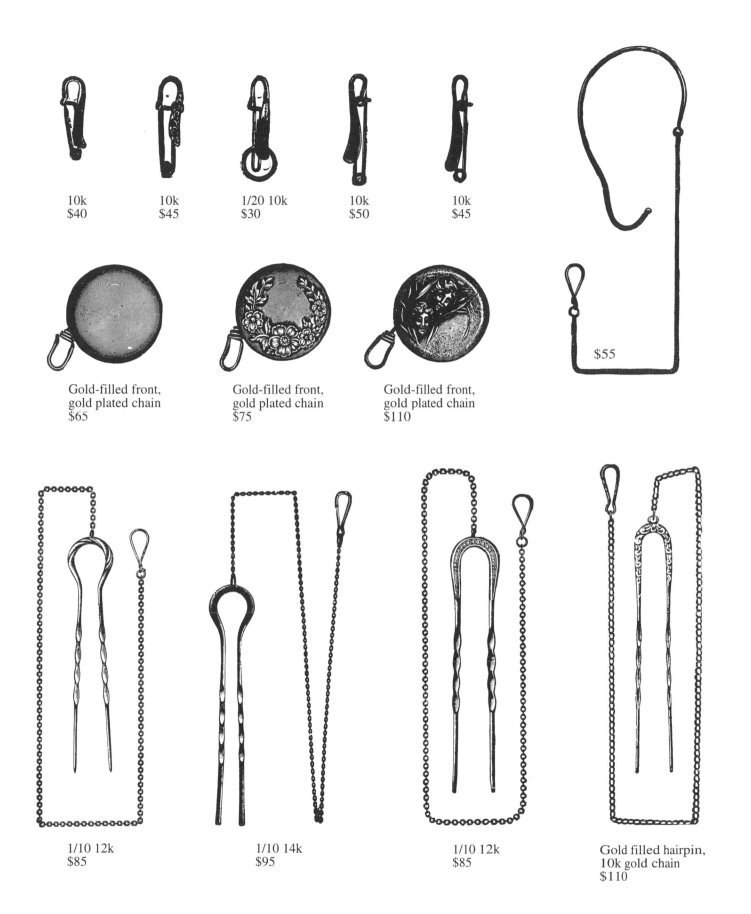

10k
$40

10k
$45

1/20 10k
$30

10k
$50

10k
$45

Gold-filled front,
gold plated chain
$65

Gold-filled front,
gold plated chain
$75

Gold-filled front,
gold plated chain
$110

$55

1/10 12k
$85

1/10 14k
$95

1/10 12k
$85

Gold filled hairpin,
10k gold chain
$110

Eyeglass chains and reels, circa 1910.

Lingerie Clasps

  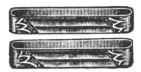

Gold-filled
$40

Gold-filled
$40

Gold-filled
$40

Solid gold front
$55

Solid gold front
$55

10 karat gold
$90

10 karat gold
$90

Solid silver
$40

Solid silver
$40

Ladies lingerie clasps. Priced as pairs.

133

Masonic and Eastern Star Jewels

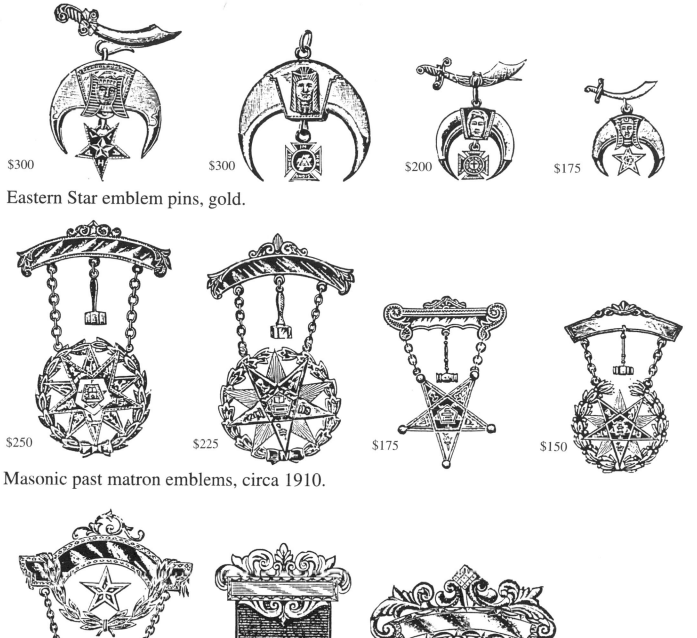

$300 $300 $200 $175

Eastern Star emblem pins, gold.

$250 $225 $175 $150

Masonic past matron emblems, circa 1910.

$1,500 $900 $1,100 $500

Past master's jewels, gold, circa 1910.   Mystic Shrine emblem charms and pins, circa 1910.

Men's Jewelry

White
gold-filled
$55

Green gold
$45

Sterling
silver
$45

Sterling
silver
$45

$40

Sterling
silver
$40

Sterling
silver
$45

This belt chain was produced in gold, gold-filled,
and sterling silver

Men's belt chains, circa 1930.

| One piece 14k plate | Lever top gold-filled | Lever top gold-filled | One piece 14k plate | Rolled gold plate | One piece 14k plate | Lever top rolled plate |

NOTE: All above $5 each

| Rolled gold plate $5 each | Lever top rolled gold plate $5 each | Rolled gold plate $5 each | Separable pearl set $8 each | Lever top pearl back $5 each | Lever top celluloid back $5 each | Separable opal celluloid back $8 each |

| Solid gold $8 each | Solid gold $8 each | Gold-filled $5 each | Lever top $5 each | White pearl $5 each | White pearl $5 each | Gold-filled $5 each |

| One piece 10k $10 each | One piece 10k $10 each | One piece 10k $10 each | One piece 10k $10 each | One piece 10k $10 each | One piece 10k $10 each | Lever top $10 each |

Collar buttons, circa 1910.

| Solid gold opal $55 | Diamond solid gold $100 | Solid gold opal $55 | Pearl solid gold $35 | Ruby solid gold $100 | Diamond cut brilliant solid gold $75 | Ruby gold $75 |

| Gold top almondine set | Opal set | Gold top chased | French pearl | White pearl top, pearl center | White pearl top | White pearl top |

Single studs, circa 1910.

| Gold-filled one piece $5 each | Gold-filled one piece $5 each | Gold-filled one piece $5 each | Lever top gold-filled $5 each | One piece gold-filled $5 each | Lever top $5 each | Pearl back $5 each |

| Solid gold back $7 each | Separable gold front $8 each | One piece 14k plate $4 each | One piece 14k plate $4 each | One piece 14k plate $4 each | One piece 14k plate $4 each | Lever top gold-filled $5 each |

Collar buttons, circa 1910.

Solid gold front
$45

Solid gold front
with fancy engraved
pattern
$55

14 karat solid gold
$45

Solid silver
$40

Solid silver
hand engraved
$35

Soft collar grip
14 karat solid gold
$75

Collar pins for soft collars.

Raised figure
$55

Solid
silver
enameled
$40

Engraved
$40

Chased
$40

Junior Am.
Mechanics
$45

Stone set
$50

Enameled
$50

Pearl barrel
gold wire and
stone set
$55

Gold
nails
$55

Pearl with
white stone
center
$45

Brilliant
set
$45

Boy's size
engraved
$40

Half chased
$55

Chased
front
$60

Raised figure
enamel top
$55

Raised
ornament
$50

Gold stone
set
$55

Stone set
$55

Gold front
onyx
$55

Gold plate
$40

Pure
aluminum
$45

Gold-filled
raised gold
ornament
$55

Gold rolled
with gold
stag
$55

Gold-filled
$45

Gold-filled
$45

Gold-filled
$45

Boy's
gold-filled
$40

Rolled
plate
$45

Enameled
sword
$45

Engraved
$45

Chased
$45

Stone set
$45

Roman color
$40

Roman
color
$40

Roman color
$40

Men's cuff buttons, circa 1895.

All above are rolled gold plate
and gold-filled unless otherwise
described. Priced as pairs.

10k solid gold
$40

10k solid gold
$45

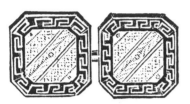  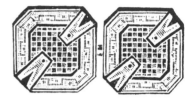

Solid silver
enamel top
$35

White metal with
cloisonne enamel top
$45

White metal with
cloisonne enamel top
$45

14k solid gold
$55

14k solid gold
$55

14k solid gold
$55

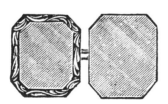  

10k solid gold
$40

10k solid gold
$40

10k solid gold
$40

Men's cuff links for soft cuffs,
circa 1910. Priced as pairs.

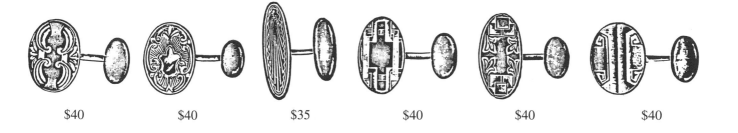

$40 $40 $35 $40 $40 $40

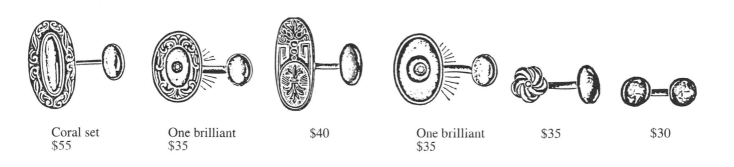

Coral set One brilliant $40 One brilliant $35 $30
$55 $35 $35

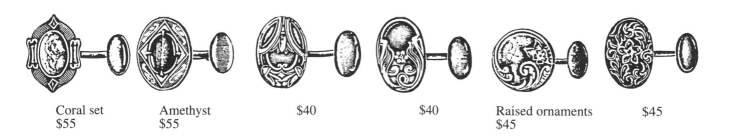

Coral set Amethyst $40 $40 Raised ornaments $45
$55 $55 $45

Gold-filled cuff link buttons,
circa 1910. Priced as pairs.

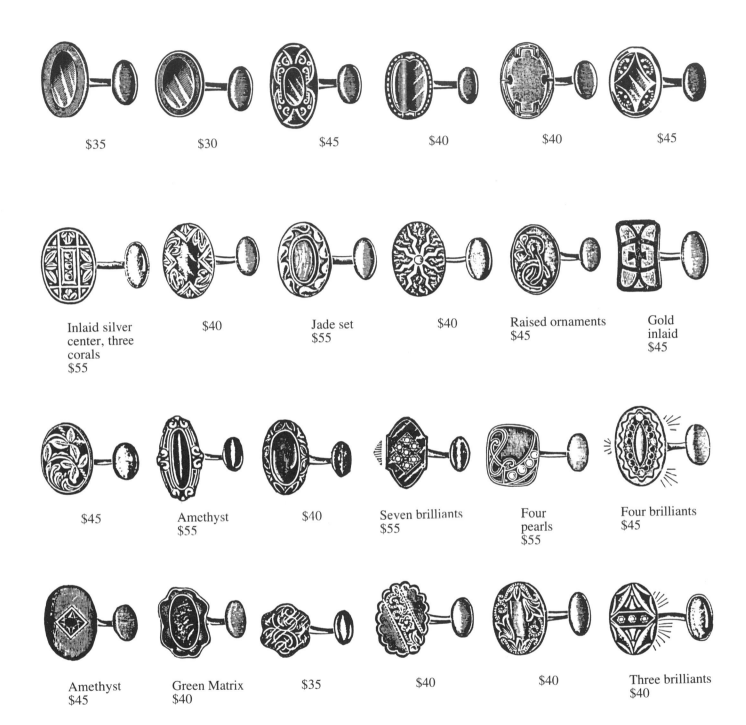

$35 $30 $45 $40 $40 $45

Inlaid silver
center, three
corals
$55

$40

Jade set
$55

$40

Raised ornaments
$45

Gold
inlaid
$45

$45

Amethyst
$55

$40

Seven brilliants
$55

Four
pearls
$55

Four brilliants
$45

Amethyst
$45

Green Matrix
$40

$35

$40

$40

Three brilliants
$40

Gold-filled cuff link buttons,
circa 1910. Priced as pairs.

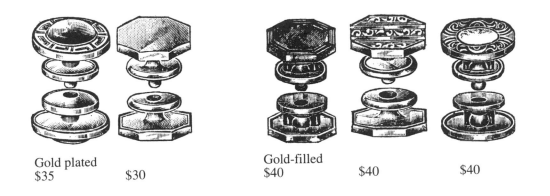

Gold plated
$35 $30

Gold-filled
$40 $40 $40

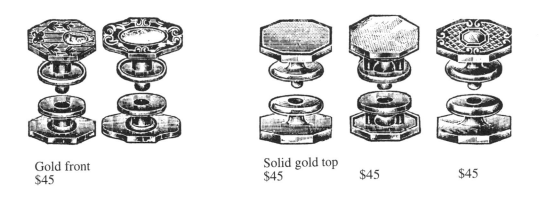

Gold front
$45

Solid gold top
$45 $45 $45

Silver plated
$30

Gold-filled
$30 $25 $30
Spool cuff links for soft cuffs

Separable cuff links popular
in the 1920s.

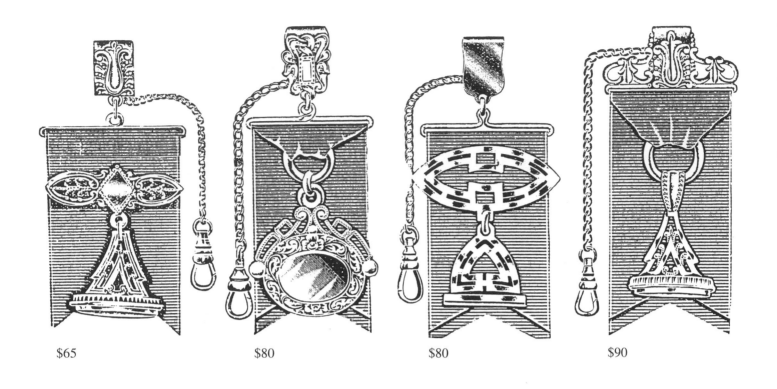

$65 $80 $80 $90

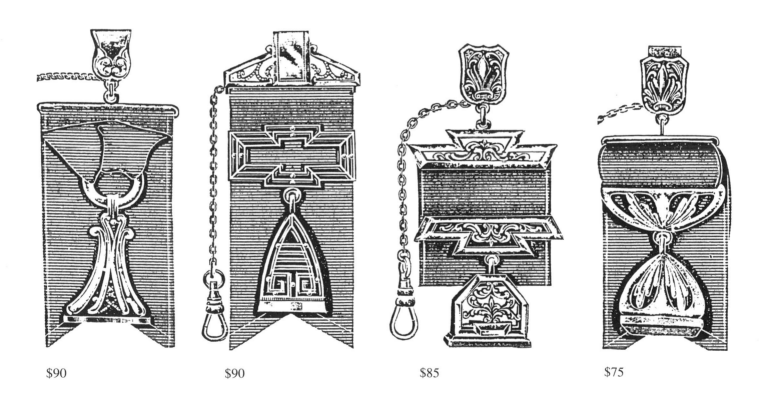

$90 $90 $85 $75

Black silk ribbon safety fobs
advertised as fine gold-filled
signet charms, circa 1910.

146

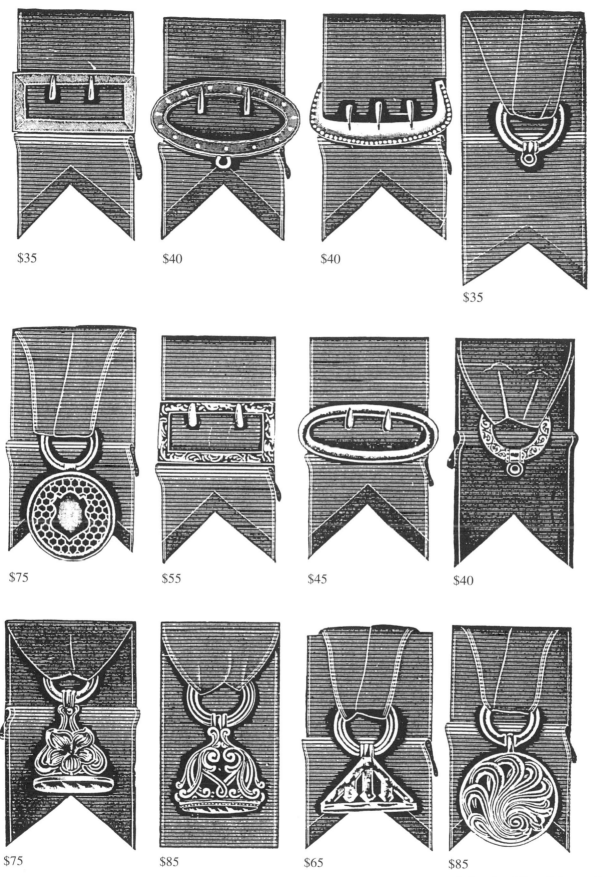

$35

$40

$40

$35

$75

$55

$45

$40

$75

$85

$65

$85

Black silk ribbon fob chains
advertised as solid gold
trimmings, circa 1910.

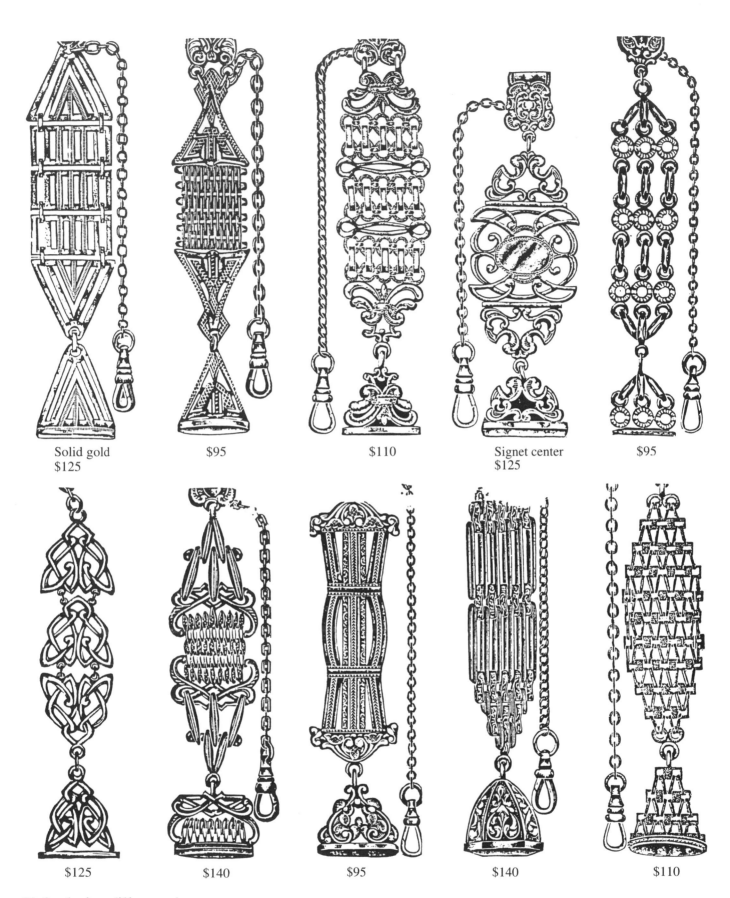

Solid gold
$125

$95

$110

Signet center
$125

$95

$125

$140

$95

$140

$110

Fob chains (illustrations are
exact size), circa 1910. All
gold-filled unless otherwise noted.

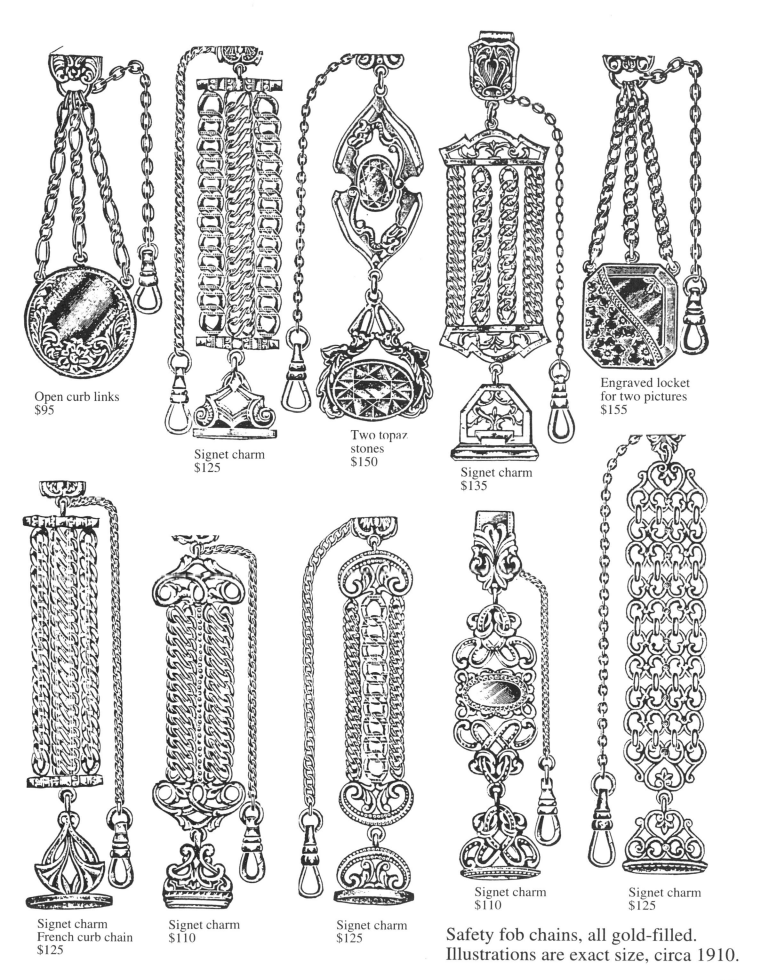

Open curb links
$95

Signet charm
$125

Two topaz
stones
$150

Signet charm
$135

Engraved locket
for two pictures
$155

Signet charm
French curb chain
$125

Signet charm
$110

Signet charm
$125

Signet charm
$110

Signet charm
$125

Safety fob chains, all gold-filled.
Illustrations are exact size, circa 1910.

Gold-filled
$25

Gold-filled
raised heads
$35

Solid gold
$35

Solid gold
$35

Solid gold
one diamond
$65

Solid gold
$40

Solid gold
$40

Gold-filled
$35

Solid gold
$35

Gold-filled
$35

Gold-filled
$40

Solid gold
$40

Solid gold
$35

Solid gold
$40

Solid gold
one brilliant
$40

Solid gold
$35

Solid gold
$35

Solid gold
raised polished signet
$40

Solid gold
$30

Solid gold
$40

Gold-filled
three brilliants
$45

Tie holders, circa 1895.

Gold-filled
$45

Gold-filled
$40

Cloisonne enamel
$65

Gold-filled
$40

Gold-filled
$45

Cloisonne enamel
$50

Gold-filled
$35

Gold-filled
$35

Sterling silver
$25

Gold-filled
$30

Gold-filled
$35

Sterling silver
$30

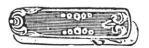
Rolled gold plate
$30

Gold-filled
$35

Sterling silver
$30

Rolled gold plate
$35

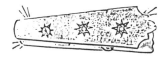
Gold-filled
$30

Sterling silver
$30

Rolled gold plate
$25

Gold-filled
$25

Sterling silver
$35

Tie holders, circa 1895

Sword Pins

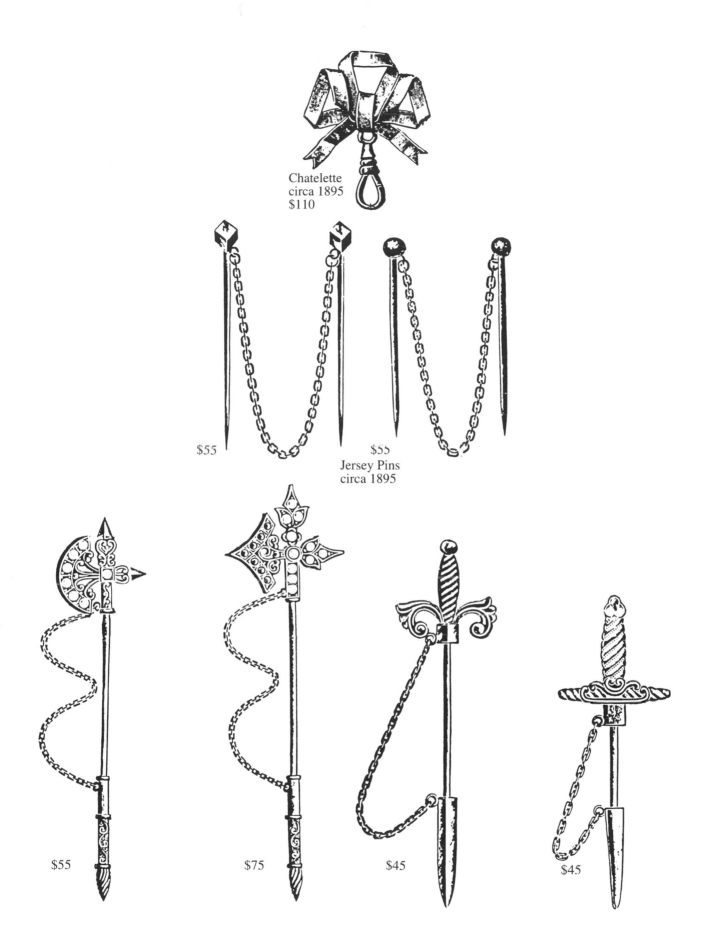

Chatelette
circa 1895
$110

$55

$55
Jersey Pins
circa 1895

$55

$75

$45

$45

Sword pins with removable scabbards, all gold-filled, circa 1895.

Appendix

Gold Marks and Weights

Gold Marks	
Gold Marks	
American	European
10k	417
14k	583
18k	750
24k	1000
Gold Abbreviations	
G.F.	gold-filled
H.G.E.	hard gold electroplated
R.G.P.	rolled gold plate
Gold Weights	
20 Pennyweights = 1 troy ounce	
12 Troy ounces = 1 pound	
Gold Alloys	
Green Gold	gold mixed with silver
Pink Gold	gold mixed with copper
White Gold	gold mixed with nickel

What does 1/20 12k mean?

It means that 1/20 (and/or 5%) of the weight of the piece of jewelry is 12k gold.

Note: The illustration shows that karat gold is covering the brass base metal on both sides, thus making it tarnish resistant.

Note: A gold-filled value is greater than a gold plated value because gold-filled has an actual layer of gold rather than a microscopic film of karat gold.

How gold-filled is created

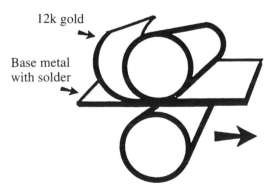

12k gold

Base metal with solder

Monogram Alphabet

A B C D E F

G H I K L M N

O P Q R S T U

V W X Y Z

Hopefully this will help
you to identify the letters
engraved on antique jewelry.

Revival Jewelry: Art Nouveau Designs

Note: These jewelry stampings (in brass) are readily
available in the 1990s from tool and dye companies
in the New England states.

Art Nouveau designs used in revival jewelry.

Wrist Watch Dial Styles
(typical of watches sold
during the 1930s)

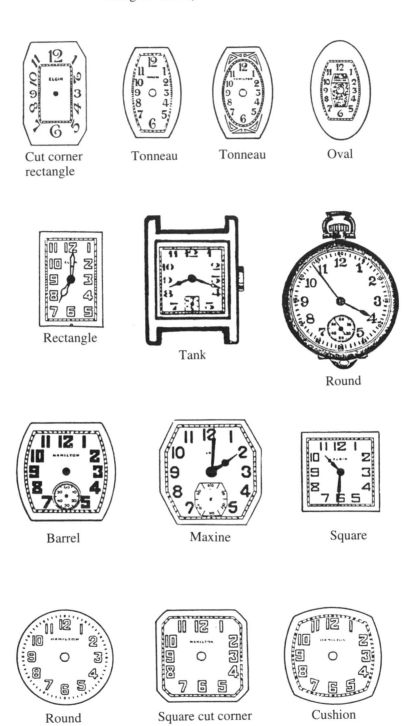

Cut corner
rectangle

Tonneau

Tonneau

Oval

Rectangle

Tank

Round

Barrel

Maxine

Square

Round

Square cut corner

Cushion

Bibliography

Catalogs

Apa Torre Del Greco, Napoli, Italy, 1978.
Busiest House in America, illustrated catalog of watches, jewelry, silverware, clocks, canes, umbrellas, 1889.
Fort Dearborn Watch and Clock Co. *Fort Dearborn Gift Book and General Catalog* (illus). Chicago, 1932.
Gatter, R.S. *Jewelry of the Better Sort.* R.S. Gatter: New York, 1910.
Mach and Co., R.H., No. 17, 1911.
Manheim and Co., H.M., New York, 1941, 1942, 1943.
Mayers Co., L.C., New York, 1940.
Marshall Field and Co. *Catalog of Jewelry and Fashions* (illus). Chicago, 1896.
Meyers Co., S.F., New York, 1910.
Montgomery Ward and Co., 1895.
---, 1902-1903.
Richardson and Co., J W. Illustrated catalog of solid gold emblems. New York, 1917-1918.
River Gems and Findings. Albuquerque, New Mexico, August 1993-July 1995.
Roddin & Co., E.V., 1895.
Sears, Roebuck, and Co., Fall 1900.
---. *Best of Sears Collectibles* 1905-1910.
---. 1915, 1923.

Books

Aswad, Ed and Michael Weinstein. *The Art and Mystique of Shell Cameos.* Florence, Alabama: Books Americana, 1991.
Baker, Lillian. *100 Years of Collectible Jewelry.* Paducah, Kentucky: Collector Books, 1995.
---. *Art Nouveau and Art Deco Jewelry.* Paducah, Kentucky: Collector Books, 1981.
Bell, Jeanenne. *Old Jewelry, 1840-1950.* 4th ed. Florence, Alabama: Books Americana, 1996.
Branson, Oscar. *What You Need to Know About Gold and Silver.* Tucson: Treasure Chest Publications Inc., 1980.
Cooksey, Shugart and Tom Engle. *The Complete Guide to American Pocket Watches.* Cleveland, Tennessee: Overstreet Publications Inc., 1986.
Cooper, Diana and Norman Battershill. *Victorian Sentimental Jewellery.* Cranberry, New Jersey: A.S. Barnes & Co. Inc., 1973.
Curran, Mona. *Collecting Antique Jewellry.* New York: Emerson Books Inc., 1970.
---. *A Treasury of Jewels and Gems.* New York: Emerson Books Inc., 1962.

Darling, Ada W. *Antique Jewelry Identification.* Leon, Iowa: Mid-Americana Book Co., 1967.
---. *Antique Jewelry Identification.* Des Moines: Wallace-Homestead Book Company, 1973.
---. *The Jeweled Trail.* Des Moines: Wallace-Homestead Book Company, 1971.
Desautels, Paul E. *The Gem Kingdom.* New York: Random House, 1971.
Dickinson, Joan Younger. *The Book of Diamonds.* New York: Avenel Books, 1965.
Echstein, J. and G. Firkins. *Gentlemen's Dress Accessories.* Buckinghamshire, England: Shire Publications, 1987.
Flower, Magaret. *Victorian Jewellery.* Cranbury, New Jersey: A.S. Barnes & Co. Inc., 1967.
Gere, Charlotte. *Victorian Jewelry Design.* Chicago: Henry Regnery Co., 1972.
Goldember, Rose Leiman. *Antique Jewelry: A Practical and Passionate Guide.* New York: Crown Publishers Inc., 1976.
Harris, Nathaniel. *Victorian Antiques.* London: Hamtpon House Productions Ltd., 1973.
Hayes, Maggie. *Maggie Hayes Jewelry Book.* New York: Van Nostrand Reinhold Company, 1972.
Henzel, S. Sylvia. *Collectible Costume Jewelry.* Rev. ed. Radnor, Pennsylvania: Wallace-Homestead Book Company, 1990.
Lewis, M.D.S. *Antique Paste Jewellery.* Boston: Boston Book and Art, 1970.
Mason, Anita. *An Illustrated Dictionary of Jewellery.* Wallop, Great Britain: Osprey Publishing Ltd., 1973.
Mebane, John. *The Complete Book of Collecting Art Nouveau.* New York: Weathervane Books, 1970.
---. *What's New That's Old.* Cranbury, New Jersey: A.S. Barnes & Co. Inc. 1969.
Meyer, Florence. *Pins for Hats and Cravats.* Des Moines: Wallace-Homestead Book Company, 1974.
McClinton, Katharine Morrison. *Antiques Past and Present.* New York: Clarkson N. Potter Inc., 1971.
Nijssen, L. Giltay. *Jewelry.* New York: Universe Books Inc., 1964.
Norbury, James. *The World of Victoriana.* New York: The Hamlyn Publishing Group Ltd., 1972.
Revi, Albert Christian. *The Spinning Wheel's Complete Book of Antiques.* New York: Grosset and Dunlap, 1977.
Sallee, Lynn. *Old Costume Jewelry.* Florence, Alabama: Books Americana, 1979.
Vandergroot, R.L. *Facets of Wealth.* Scottsdale, Arizona: Palladian House, 1976.
Whitlock, Herbert P. *The Story of Gems.* New York: Emerson Books Inc., 1970.

Index